TRAVELER'S GUIDE TO THE GREAT SIOUX WAR

TRAVELER'S GUIDE TO THE GREAT SIOUX WAR

THE BATTLEFIELDS, FORTS, AND RELATED SITES OF AMERICA'S GREATEST INDIAN WAR

BY PAUL L. HEDREN

Montana Historical Society Press
Helena, Montana

Cover image: Last Stand Hill at Little Bighorn Battlefield National Monument, by ChuckHaney.com

Back cover image: Veterans of the Great Sioux War pose on the Little Bighorn Battlefield in 1926, the last great anniversary welcoming so many battle and war survivors. Left to right: Joseph M. T. Partello (Fifth Infantry, 1879), White Man Runs Him (Crow scout, 1876), Edward S. Godfrey (Seventh Cavalry, 1876), and Max Big Man (Crow cultural interpreter). Edwin L. Wisherd/ National Geographic Image Collection

Cover design: Eric Pasha Hanson, epashhansdesign.com

Book design: Kathryn Fehlig, fehligdesign.com

Typeset in Copperplate and Goudy

Printed by Sheridan Books, Chelsea, Michigan

Distributed by the Globe Pequot Press, 46 Goose Lane, Guilford, Connecticut 06437 (800) 243-0495

08 09 10 11 12 13 14 15 16 17   4 5 6 7 8 9 10 11 12 13 14

Library of Congress Cataloging-in-Publication Data

Hedren, Paul L.
  Traveler's guide to the Great Sioux War: the battlefields, forts, and related sites of America's greatest Indian war / by Paul L. Hedren.
      p. cm.
    Includes bibliographical references and index.
    ISBN-13: 978-0-917298-38-7
    ISBN-10: 0-917298-38-1
    1. Dakota Indians—Wars, 1876. 2. Cheyenne Indians—Wars, 1876. 3. Battlefields—Great Plains—Guidebooks. 4. Great Plains—Guidebooks.
  I. Title.
  E83.876.H42 1996   95–43026
  978'.02—dc20   CIP

Traveler's Guide to the Great Sioux War was made possible in part by funding provided by the Federal Highway Administration and the Montana Department of Transportation through an agreement with the State Historic Preservation Office and the Advisory Council on Historic Preservation.

CONTENTS

MAPS

GREAT SIOUX WAR SITES
BY STATE AND PROVINCE

Acknowledgments

This revised edition of *Traveler's Guide to the Great Sioux War* updates some thirty matters that have changed in the guide or on the Sioux War Trail since the book first appeared in 1996. In several instances, directional details required updating. Some sites now feature new monuments or developments that warranted mention. And, regrettably, one critical field has closed to general visitation, a matter carefully noted.

As I undertook this project initially, I was pleased to recognize the support of friends who aided the effort, and the list continues to grow. I thank kindly Tom Buecker, Ephriam Dickson III, Marilyn Grant, Sherry Graves, Jerry Greene, Pete Hart, Greg Hennessy, Paul Hutton, Marv Kaiser, Roye Lindsay, Doug McChristian, Jack McDermott, Chuck Rankin, Tom Wilder, and the late James Willert.

An array of individuals and institutions permitted the use of important images from their collections, including James Brust; John Carter, Nebraska State Historical Society; James Crain; Lory Morrow, Kirby Lambert, and Dianne Keller, Montana Historical Society; Larry Ness; State Historical Society of North Dakota; John Popovich; and LaVera Rose, South Dakota State Historical Society. Several other contributors are noted in respective photo credits.

The Montana Historical Society rendered extraordinary support then and now, and I gratefully remember Martha Kohl, Glenda Bradshaw, Tammy Ryan, Kathryn Fehlig, and Doug O'looney for assistance rendered initially; and Molly Holz, the Press's current editor, who warmly encouraged this new edition; Glenda Bradshaw, the Press's indefatigable photo editor; and Beverly Magley of Edit-Write LLC, who cheerfully and skillfully shepherded this updated edition.

Lastly, I care to acknowledge my patient wife, Connie, who's visiting most of these sites for the first time, daughters Ethne and Whitney, who have seen them all already, and granddaughters Emma and Kate, who give reason to traipse again across the northern plains, as if, Connie would say, I needed an excuse.

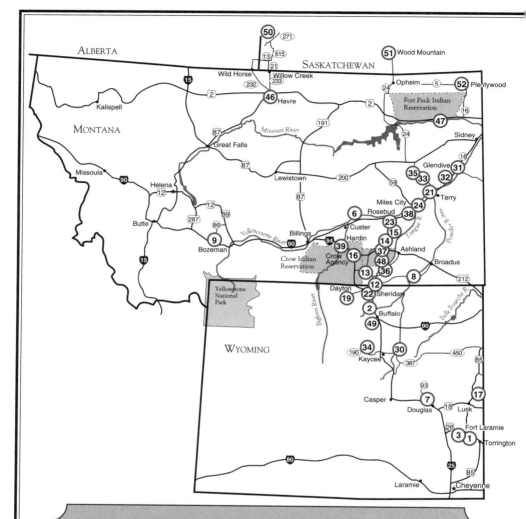

OVERVIEW OF SIOUX WAR COUNTRY

This map is included to show the approximate location of every site featured in this guide. Site numbers are keyed to the table of contents and to the numbered "Getting There" entries highlighted in gray throughout the text.

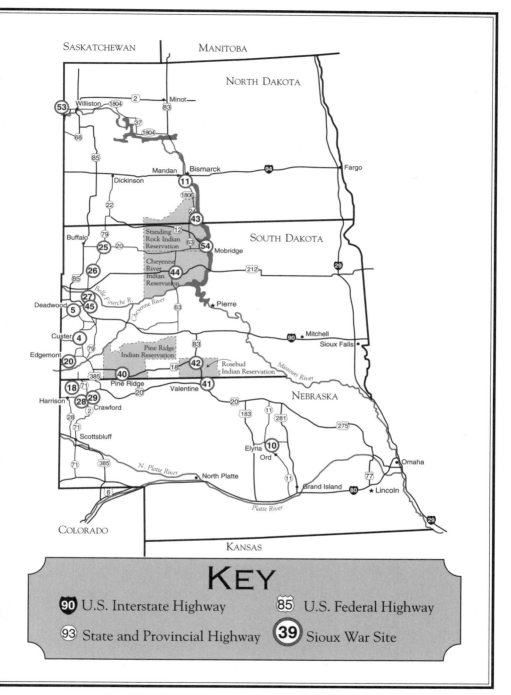

SASKATCHEWAN   MANITOBA

NORTH DAKOTA

53 Williston 1804 2 Minot
                        83
         37
68   1804
      85

      22   Mandan Bismarck 94   Fargo
                Dickinson   11
                          1806
                        24
Buffalo 79   12 43
      25 20   Standing   63 54   SOUTH DAKOTA
26   Rock Indian   Mobridge
85   Reservation
                Cheyenne   212   29
27   River 44
Deadwood 45   Indian
5   Reservation
Custer 4   63   Pierre
Edgemont   79
20   Pine Ridge   83   90 Mitchell
        385   Indian Reservation   Sioux Falls
18 71   18 42   Rosebud
        40   Indian Reservation Missouri River
28 29   Pine Ridge Valentine 41
Harrison 28 2 Crawford 20   NEBRASKA
        71   20
                    183 11
Scottsbluff   281 275
71 385   77   Omaha
        N. Platte River   Elyria 10   80
                    Ord   Grand Island Lincoln
6   North Platte 11
COLORADO   Platte River   29

KANSAS

KEY

90 U.S. Interstate Highway   85 U.S. Federal Highway

93 State and Provincial Highway   39 Sioux War Site

INTRODUCTION

THE GREAT SIOUX WAR OF 1876–77 was America's most prolonged and costly Indian war, and it remains a century later still its most alluring. Waged over the glitter of Black Hills gold, and whether the rights and privileges guaranteed the Lakota, or Sioux Indians, by the Fort Laramie Treaty of 1868 were inviolate, the war transformed the entire northern plains from Indian and buffalo country to the domain of miners, cattle-men, and settlers.

The Great Sioux War mixed high drama, pathos, and extraordinary individual and collective effort. Consider the enigma of Custer and the Seventh Cavalry at the Little Bighorn [16]; the devastation befalling the Northern Cheyennes on the Red Fork of the Powder River [34]; the sense-less killing of Crazy Horse at Camp Robinson [28]; and the irony of Sitting Bull's surrender at Fort Buford [53]. Add a score of other battlefields and forts, an Indian reservation larger than the State of Pennsylvania, and a war zone spanning five states, and the sum is a military-cultural epic with little parallel in American history.

The magnetism of the sites alone is phenomenal. Each year more than 425,000 visitors stream to the Little Bighorn battlefield [16] in southeastern Montana. Annual visitation at the partially reconstructed Fort Abraham Lincoln [11], south of Mandan, North Dakota, is equally dramatic, and so are visitor numbers at Fort Robinson, Nebraska [28], and Fort Laramie, Wyoming [3].

In part, the vast geography of the Great Sioux War intensifies its lure. The Great Sioux Reservation, created by the Fort Laramie Treaty of 1868, spanned all of present-day South Dakota laying west of the Missouri River. The additional buffalo hunting territory accorded the Lakota stretched southward across Nebraska to the Republican River, and westward across

Wyoming to the Bighorn Mountains. The sum comprised a vast, rich prairie that sustained the great northern bison herd and untold elk and deer and provided a larder that had nourished the Plains Indian tribes for centuries. As well, this landscape held mineral and other riches that beckoned whites in the late nineteenth century and ultimately pitted two cultures in a war of will and transition.

For the army, the northern plains embraced three administrative jurisdictions. From his headquarters in Chicago, Lieutenant General Philip H. Sheridan commanded the Military Division of the Missouri, overseeing all military operations in the plains territory and beyond. On the northern tier, Sheridan's Division of the Missouri encompassed two administrative subdistricts. From St. Paul, Brigadier General Alfred H. Terry commanded the Department of Dakota, comprising the State of Minnesota and the vast Dakota and Montana territories. From Omaha, Brigadier General George Crook commanded the Department of the Platte, embracing the states of Iowa and Nebraska, and the territories of Wyoming and Utah, plus a corner of Idaho. Within these two departments lay the Great Sioux Reservation, the extended buffalo hunting lands, the Black Hills, five Sioux agencies, twenty-five military posts (with others to be added), two railroads, and a dozen vital rivers.

The Great Sioux War bloodied twenty-two different fields in what is present-day Nebraska, Wyoming, South Dakota, North Dakota, and Montana.* Today, many sites manifest commemorative monuments, most erected early in this century by historians and community partisans fearful that these intriguing fields might be forgotten. The Little Bighorn battlefield, long commonly known as Custer's battlefield [16], received

---

*Fort Pease, February–March 1876; Powder River, March 5, 1876; Powder River, March 17, 1876; Grace Creek, April 28, 1876; Tongue River, June 9, 1876; Rosebud Creek, June 17, 1876; Little Bighorn, June 25–26, 1876; Tongue River, July 7, 1876; Warbonnet Creek, July 17, 1876; Powder River, August 2, 1876; Rosebud Creek, August 2, 1876; Yellowstone River, August 23, 1876; Slim Buttes, September 9–10, 1876; Owl Creek, September 14, 1876; Richard Creek, October 14, 1876; Clear Creek, October 15, 1876; Cedar Creek, October 21, 1876; Powder River, November 25, 1876; Wolf Mountains, January 8, 1877; Elkhorn Creek, January 12, 1877; Crow Creek, February 23, 1877; Little Muddy Creek, May 7, 1877.

initial federal protection as early as 1879 when it was declared a national cemetery. Today it is a national monument administered by the National Park Service. As well, the nearby Rosebud battlefield [13] is a Montana state monument. Some war forts are equally well protected. Fort Abraham Lincoln [11] is North Dakota's premier state park, as Fort Robinson [28] is Nebraska's. Fort Laramie [3] is a national historic site administered by the National Park Service. In Wyoming, Fort Fetterman [7] is a state historic site, as is Fort Buford [53] in North Dakota.

Virtually every principal landmark associated with the Great Sioux War is accessible by modern automobile. Hard pavement and good directional signing lead to the better-known sites, and all-weather roads are the norm in nearly every other instance. And each site is worth viewing, with the Little Bighorn battlefield [16] still invoking a sense of mystery, the reconstructed guardhouse at Fort Robinson [28] a sense of rage, and all places expressing the costs paid by both sides as Euramericans wrested the northern plains from the Sioux and the buffalo.

This, then, is a traveler's guide to the Great Sioux War, fashioned so that the modern-day motorist can access the battlefields, forts, and landscapes of one of the West's most enduring dramas.

HOW TO USE THIS GUIDE

THE *TRAVELER'S GUIDE TO THE GREAT SIOUX WAR* opens by surveying geographical and political contexts of the war. Thereafter, the *Guide* presents the story chronologically, from opening actions in the spring of 1876, through the death of Crazy Horse in September 1877 and the distant surrender of Sitting Bull in 1881. The narrative is broken by numbered GETTING THERE entries describing fifty-four locations critical to the Sioux War story. These highlighted texts describe respective battle and skirmish sites, forts, and landmarks as seen today, and provide essential directions for public access by vehicle. In every instance, directions are keyed to official highway maps provided by respective states and province. Wherever a site is discussed in the text, its first mention in each paragraph is keyed to its GETTING THERE entry by number; these numbers are also used to mark sites on five maps: a map showing all of the Sioux War sites discussed in this guide; and four maps tracing the war's most significant campaign trails.

The inclusion and exclusion of Sioux War sites was subjective, but logical. While every principal battlefield and skirmish site associated with the war gained inclusion, less automatic were the array of ancillary sites. For instance, if the various military forts located in the Dakota and Platte departments yielded garrisons alone, as did virtually every post in Terry's and Crook's control, but thereafter played no greater role in the conflict, the sites were not necessarily included in the *Guide*. Neither were the army's administrative headquarters in Chicago, St. Paul, and Omaha. But forts on the margins of the war zone inevitably had additional roles of support and supply and were necessarily included. In the instance of the

Black Hills gold country, site inclusion was limited to Custer City [4] and Deadwood [5], both being excellent examples of the 1876 gold rush genre. The identity of specific Indian sites was more difficult to determine, but several Indian landmarks are included, as are the Lakota and Northern Cheyenne agencies and reservations of the postwar era.

CAUTION: Ownership of Great Sioux War sites is mixed. The rights of private landowners need always be observed and respected, and the courtesy of asking permission first often yields access. Federal and state preservation laws protect many of the Sioux War sites, and the collecting of artifacts on any of them is both unethical and invariably unlawful.

Powder River Country, Central Wyoming.
The combination of rolling prairie and regular water courses like the Powder River, seen here in central Wyoming, proved an ideal landscape for nomadic Indian tribes like the Lakotas and Northern Cheyennes.

CHAPTER I
AN ORIENTATION TOUR THROUGH THE SIOUX WAR LANDSCAPE

TO KNOW AND APPRECIATE THE GEOGRAPHY of the northern plains is to understand why the Lakota and Northern Cheyenne Indians and the other northern tribes cherished this rich, diverse landscape. Though often described simply as plains country, in reality the territory in which the Great Sioux War was fought was a remarkably varied landscape unified throughout by the vast, rolling prairie.

The grasslands of old are perhaps best seen in northeastern Wyoming. This region, in part, is what the army labeled the "Powder River country," since it drained the Powder and its innumerable small tributaries. Herds of buffalo grazed this undulating sea of grass and sage, luring the Sioux and other nomadic hunters on their seasonal quests. As well, the prairie landscape was a diverse haunt for deer and game birds. Water was reliably found in the major drainages, and in widened valleys, copses of cottonwood trees provided shelter and fuel. In all the United States, the original buffalo herds survived longest in the Powder River country and the adjoining Big Open of central Montana, and to see this vast sea of grass today is to appreciate its understated beauty and glimpse the Plains Indians' connection to the natural world. As the prospect of conflict broke across the northern plains in the mid-1870s, envision, as well, government emissaries coming first to this very countryside in winter, hoping to avert a war.

As one ventures north into southeastern Montana, the landscape changes markedly. Wildlife is plentiful there, as well, and the valleys of the Yellowstone, Bighorn, Tongue, and Powder rivers are broad and lush. But Montana's southeastern uplands are more rugged and timber covered, with pines and cedars. Though not truly mountainous, craggy highlands

Montana Historical Society Photograph Archives

Buffalo Grazing the "Big Open."
In this L. A. Huffman photograph from 1880, buffalo still graze the Montana landscape north of the Yellowstone River. This great northern herd did not survive much longer, but in the mid-1870s the animals powerfully beckoned the Lakotas.

like the Wolf Mountains [36] have become legendary in the Sioux War story. This was prime buffalo country, too. Perhaps as a result of its greater physical diversity and natural lure, more Sioux War battles were fought in southeastern Montana than any other locale in the war zone.

The prairies of western North and South Dakota exhibit drier and flatter qualities than adjoining Wyoming and Montana. But this was still good hunting country, particularly in the so-called "badlands" comprising the drainage of the Little Missouri River. Not to be confused with the South Dakota badlands, the North Dakota, or Little Missouri, badlands offered a ruggedness that was a haven to wildlife and the nomadic tribes. But just east of the Little Missouri River the land turns parched and is more scantily vegetated. General Crook's infamous "mud," or "starvation," march [26] occurred while crossing this daunting, almost lunar-like, Dakota prairie.

The most spectacular natural anomaly on the northern plains is the Black Hills of western South Dakota. Revered by the Lakota and Cheyenne Indians as sacred country, the Black Hills were mineral and timber rich.

Their opening and settlement was a principal issue of the Great Sioux War. Still enticing, the Black Hills's chief industry today is tourism. Though gambling, snake pits, and carved mountains beckon, so does the area's reverent natural beauty and its mining roots, both subtly surviving and harkening the hard-fought Indian war of 1876–77.

Today, America's interstate highways are the great avenues leading to Sioux War country. Whether by Interstate 25, 80, 90, or 94, or the innumerable primary and secondary routes between, a sense of the beauty and complexity of the northern plains landscape can be gained by a three- or four-day circle drive through its midst. The entrances, exits, and pauses given here are arbitrary.

Start at Douglas, Wyoming, and travel north to Gillette on Wyoming 59, continuing to Sheridan, Wyoming, on U.S. 14. This route spans the Powder River country, the finest of the Sioux and buffalo lair. As well, one crosses Crook's campaign trails repeatedly.

From Sheridan, travel Interstate 90 north to Crow Agency, Montana, traversing portions of the 1860s Bozeman Trail [2], used as a military road in 1876, and the land between the prairies and Bighorn Mountains. General Crook's summer traces [13, 19, 22] quickly transit to Custer and Reno, and scenes of their fateful battle on June 25, 1876 [16].

From Crow Agency, travel east on U.S. 212 to Lame Deer, Montana, and from there turn north on Montana 39 to Forsyth. Continue eastbound on Interstate 94 to Belfield, North Dakota. This traverse exposes the diverse landscape of the Yellowstone basin, from its timbered highlands to its navigable stream beds. That portion of the interstate in North Dakota closely parallels Terry's and Custer's campaign trail of May 1876, and Crook's exiting route of August. As well, the route passes the Theodore Roosevelt National Park, where buffalo, elk, and deer still abound in a vast prairie landscape that is among the most dramatic and least impaired on the entire northern plains.

From Belfield, North Dakota, turn south on U.S. 85 to Buffalo, South Dakota, and then east on South Dakota 20 to Reva. At Reva turn south on South Dakota 79, traveling to Sturgis. These highways closely approximate the route of Crook's starvation march [26] into the Black Hills, and at midpoint cross an angling escarpment known as Slim Buttes [25]. This expanse is another wonderfully unobstructed landscape.

The proclaimed intent of the campaign was to move the roaming Sioux to their reservation, but after the battle of the Little Bighorn, the original reservation boundaries became invisible. Ironically, then, the historic Great Sioux Reservation begins at the North Dakota–South Dakota border, and the Slim Buttes battlefield [25] at Reva lies distinctly within original reservation boundaries.

Finally, travel South Dakota 34 from Sturgis to Deadwood [5], and U.S. 385 from Deadwood south through the heart of the Black Hills. Evidences of the great gold rush abound, though rarely, it seems, do modern-day tourism promoters connect the mining events of 1876 with the Indian war that occurred in consequence.

This three- maybe four-day travel is recommended solely for the purpose of gaining an appreciation of Sioux War geography. Prairies can be dissimilar and so too their uplands and bottoms. Remarkably, however, in its entirety, this was once Lakota and Cheyenne Indian country and the natural lair of millions of buffalo, deer, and antelope. And for eighteen months in 1876 and 1877, this was the setting for the greatest Indian conflict ever to occur in America.

CHAPTER II
SETTING THE STAGE

IN LARGE MEASURE, THE GREAT SIOUX WAR of 1876–77 culminated a generation of strife between the Western Sioux and seemingly endless waves of Euramericans advancing to destinations beyond the plains. Predictably, the emigrants demanded government safeguarding of their travels, and at Fort Laramie [3] in 1851 a great treaty was signed to assure that passage. However well intended, the first Fort Laramie, or Horse Creek, Treaty never achieved a meaningful peace. Though blood was shed before the infamous Grattan fight [1] of August 19, 1854, never before had killing been so wanton in the Trans-Mississippi West. At day's end an entire command of Regular Army soldiers, led by youthful Brevet Second Lieutenant

Grattan Fight Marker. *This small monument marks the Grattan bloodshed of August 19, 1854. The fighting occurred in what are corn and sugar beet fields today, midway between the monument and the distant North Platte River.*

John L. Grattan, Sixth Infantry, lay dead, having foolishly marched into Conquering Bear's Brule Lakota village near the fort while attempting to placate the demands of a passing emigrant.

GETTING
THERE

1

Grattan Battlefield, Wyoming

The Grattan fight of August 19, 1854, heralded a generation of fighting between Lakota Indians and the U.S. Army. No soldiers survived this devastating encounter. The Grattan battlefield and marker is midway between Fort Laramie and Lingle, on the south side of the North Platte River. From Fort Laramie, go east five miles on U.S. 26, then south two and east two miles on Wyoming 157. This is private property.

TRAVELER'S TIP: Fort Laramie National Historic Site [3] is nearby.

THE GOVERNMENT'S RETALIATION for Grattan's killing was swift. In September 1855 Colonel William S. Harney of the Second Dragoons led a command of infantry, artillery, and dragoons against a Lakota village encamped on Blue Water Creek, Nebraska. Some eighty-six Indians were killed. Fighting further intensified during the Civil War years, especially in the wake of perversions like the Sand Creek massacre in Colorado, where volunteer troops slaughtered more than two hundred Cheyenne Indians, who had signaled their peaceful intentions by raising a U.S. flag over their camp, and the punitive Powder River Expedition in Wyoming, aimed at clearing the way for new roads to Montana's goldfields.

The discovery of gold in western Montana in 1862 brought a fresh focus to northern plains Indian relations, particularly when, for the first time, a new trail northward from Fort Laramie [3] bisected the luxurious Powder River country. When the United States Army garrisoned this Bozeman Trail [2] in the summer of 1866, trouble was guaranteed. Under Red Cloud's leadership, Sioux resistance to the invasion was so formidable that the trail barely functioned as a miner's thoroughfare, and the soldier garrisons at forts Reno, Phil Kearny, and C. F. Smith lived under perpetual siege. The hallmark Sioux battles of the 1850s paled against the slaughter of Captain William J. Fetterman's command on December 21, 1866, three miles north of Fort Phil Kearny [2] and the intensity of the

Hayfield Fight near Fort C. F. Smith and the Wagon Box Fight at Phil Kearny's pinery, eight months later.

GETTING THERE **2**

Fort Phil Kearny, Fetterman Battlefield, and Bozeman Trail, Wyoming-Montana

The story of Red Cloud's successful resistance to the short-lived Bozeman Trail, which connected Fort Laramie and the Montana gold-fields, is best told at the Fort Phil Kearny State Historic Site located just off Interstate 90 midway between Buffalo and Sheridan, Wyoming. A small museum interprets the fort's brief but bloody history. Three miles north on U.S. 87 is the Fetterman battlefield, commemorated by a dramatic monument erected in 1908. Directions to other significant Bozeman Trail landmarks in Wyoming and Montana can be obtained at the Fort Phil Kearny museum.

TRAVELER'S TIP: Crook's Camp Cloud Peak [22] and Fort McKinney [49] are nearby.

Fetterman Monument.
This striking rock monument beside U.S. 87, several miles north of the Fort Phil Kearny State Historic Site, commemorates the 1866 wintertime battle between Red Cloud's Sioux warriors and soldiers of the Eighteenth Infantry commanded by William Fetterman.

National Archives

Fort Laramie in 1877 (above).
Stanton Expedition photographer Charles Howard captured at midyear this Sioux War–era image of Fort Laramie, nestled along a bend of the Laramie River one mile from its confluence with the North Platte.

Fort Laramie Iron Bridge (below).
This iron bridge, erected in 1875 across the North Platte River, survives in immaculate condition as a prominent feature of the Fort Laramie National Historic Site. Thousands of Black Hills–bound miners crossed the bridge in 1875 and 1876, as did General Crook and the men of his successive expeditions against the Sioux.

Fort Laramie Cavalry Barrack.
*The Fort Laramie site preserves an extraordinary array of
historical resources, including nearly two dozen original
army buildings spanning the fort's existence from 1849
to 1890. This original two-company, two-story cavalry
barrack constructed in 1875 is a one-of-a-kind structure
in the American West. The southern half of the barrack
is meticulously refurnished to depict the residency of
Company K, Second Cavalry, in mid-1876. Commanded
by Captain James Egan, Company K played a prolonged role
in the Great Sioux War.*

SIOUX ATTACKS FORCED THE GOVERNMENT to close the Bozeman
Trail [2], which soon was to be replaced by the transcontinental railroad
and the Montana Trail anyway. The document closing the trail and thus
ostensibly ending Red Cloud's War, a sixteen-page parchment known as
the Fort Laramie Treaty of 1868, proved no more effective than the 1851
compact and, in fact, provided underpinnings for other fractious relations
between whites and the Sioux that boiled continuously in the 1870s and
reverberate even to this day.

At face value, the seventeen articles of the Fort Laramie Treaty were
crafted to transform the Teton Sioux from nomadic buffalo hunters into
Christian farmers. One important article created the Great Sioux Reservation which, despite its vastness, actually represented a diminution of
traditional Sioux territory. In the midst of the reservation lay the Black
Hills, which in 1868 were little appreciated by whites and barely explored.
As well, the Fort Laramie Treaty provided vast tracts of land in Wyoming

Squad Room, Fort Laramie Cavalry Barrack.
Contrary to modern-day notions of romance and adventure in the so-called Indian Fighting Army, life in the cavalry and infantry was a rather base existence. This squad room was home to fifty or sixty men. Privacy was nonexistent, and life was regulated from sunup to sundown. Despite the danger, field service in the Great Sioux War was generally welcomed by the enlisted men as an escape from garrison routines.

and Nebraska for the continued hunting of buffalo. These so-called "unceded lands" could not be settled by whites, but they were not intended as permanent residences for Indians either. However well intentioned, the Fort Laramie Treaty bought no peace and did little to acculturate the Sioux.

For one thing, the Fort Laramie Treaty commissioners hardly could have anticipated the Panic of 1873, which halted the advance of the Northern Pacific Railroad at Bismarck, North Dakota, and made the glimmer of Black Hills gold irresistible to hard-luck Americans. George Custer's Black Hills Expedition in 1874 confirmed long-held rumors of gold in Sioux country, and a second surveying expedition from Fort Laramie [3] to the Hills in 1875 substantiated the reports. Though the advance of the Northern Pacific Railroad, the sanctity of the hunting lands, and the effectiveness of acculturation were among the fundamental issues of the Great Sioux War, none exceeded the impact of gold in the Black Hills as a precipitator of war and a justification for settling what was then being called the "Sioux problem."

Remarkably, Fort Laramie [3] had already witnessed a generation of strife between the Sioux and whites, and the Black Hills gold rush brought the post to center stage once again. Key to the fort's pivotal role in 1875 and 1876 was its well-established position on the trail connecting the Union Pacific Railroad at Cheyenne, Wyoming, and the goldfields to the north and the Sioux agencies of Nebraska to the northeast. Increasing the fort's significance was its new iron bridge spanning the North Platte River, the greatest natural barrier to Black Hills gold.

GETTING THERE [3]

Fort Laramie, Wyoming

Fort Laramie was the only military post in Sioux War country to combine a formidable garrison, excellent roads to vital destinations, and a substantial bridge across the greatest natural barrier en route; these elements allowed the post to become a significant staging area for the U.S. Army during the conflict.

The Fort Laramie National Historic Site is located three miles southwest of the small town of Fort Laramie on Wyoming 160. Many original buildings survive, and most are refurnished to reflect important eras in the fort's history. The 1875 Fort Laramie bridge across the North Platte River also survives, meticulously preserved by the National Park Service. Reminders of the Great Sioux War abound, particularly in the painstaking restoration and refurnishing of the fort's two-company cavalry barrack to reflect the occupancy of a Second Cavalry company in mid-1876.

TRAVELER'S TIP: The Grattan battlefield [1] is nearby.

WITH THE BLACK HILLS INVASION COMING principally from the south, it followed that the development of the goldfields was chiefly a south-to-north pursuit. Initial gold discoveries occurred along French Creek in the south-central Black Hills, and miners hutted themselves there during the winter of 1874–75, only to be removed by a Fort Laramie [3] squadron early in 1875. Custer City [4] was platted along French Creek in mid-1875, and grew to as many as six thousand residents that winter, though the population waned to five or six hundred by mid-1876.

Gordon Stockade.

The Gordon Stockade east of Custer commemorates the brief occupation of the Gordon-Russell-Collins party during the winter of 1874–75. They had invaded the Black Hills shortly after the Custer expedition pronounced gold among the grass roots but were expelled by troops from Fort Laramie in April 1875. This modern reconstruction is based upon archaeological and photographic evidence.

4 GETTING THERE

Custer City, South Dakota

The 1875 gold rush town of Custer is some forty miles southwest of Rapid City at the junction of U.S. 385 and U.S. 16. Evidence of the lure of gold digging abounds in the town and its rural neighborhoods and in several museums and roadside markers. The reconstructed Gordon Stockade, occupied by miners in 1874–75, is four miles east on U.S. Alt 16. Crook's men passed through in the fall of 1876 en route to Camp Robinson [28] and the termination of their campaign. A sobering reminder of their journey is seen three miles east of town at a lone soldier grave marker recalling the death of Private John Pommer of the Fifth Cavalry.

Courtesy of Jim Crain

Black Hills Miners.
*In this 1876 photograph by D. S. Mitchell, placer miners
are seen working a gulch near Deadwood. The placer claims
were rich but short-lived, succeeded by hard rock prospects
like the legendary Homestake Mine.*

PROCLAMATION !!!

WHEREAS the President of the United States has directed that no miners, or other unauthorized citizens, be allowed to remain in the Indian reservation of the Black Hills, or in the unceded territory to the west, until some new treaty arrangements have been made with the Indians:

And WHEREAS, by the same authority, the undersigned is directed to occupy said reservation and territory with troops, and to remove all miners and other unauthorized citizens, who may be now, or may hereafter come into this country in violation of the treaty obligations :—

Therefore, the undersigned hereby requires every miner and other unauthorized citizen to leave the territory known as the Black Hills, the Powder river, and Big Horn country by and before the 15th day of August next.

He hopes that the good sense and law abiding disposition of the miners will prompt them to obey this order without compelling a resort to force.

It is suggested that the miners, now in the hills, assemble at the military post about to be established at Camp Harney, near the stockade on French creek, on or before the 10th day of August.

That they, then and there hold a meeting, and take such steps as may seem best to them, by organization and drafting of proper resolutions, to secure to each, when this country shall have been opened, the benefit of his discoveries and the labor he has expended.

(Signed) GEORGE CROOK,

Brigadier General, U. S. A ,
Com'g Dep't of the Platte.

Camp Crook, D. T.,
July 29, 1875.

Crook's Black Hills Proclamation.

Forced by the Fort Laramie Treaty to expel invading miners, Brigadier General Crook distributed copies of this eight-by-ten-inch proclamation throughout the diggings. Some miners heeded this legitimate attempt to control the stampede, but many more simply evaded the army's patrols and continued their quest. The Black Hills goldfields were unofficially opened in November 1875 when President Grant withdrew the policing troops.

BY THE SUMMER OF 1876 the focus of the Black Hills gold rush had shifted to the northern hills, where the diggings featured extensive placer and hard rock prospects. Quickly Deadwood [5], Whitewood, and nearby Crook City, all located on Whitewood Creek, emerged as centers of feverish activity, and Deadwood, with some fifty-five hundred residents emerged as the largest community in the Black Hills. Common talk in the mining communities was of the peril posed by Indians and desperados as the "Hillers" traveled to and from the diggings. The two most popular Black Hills newspapers, the Cheyenne *Daily Leader* and Deadwood's *Black Hills Pioneer*, regularly featured correspondents' reports from the war front and tales of woe experienced on the trails. News in the early Black Hills, it seems, was limited to gold and the Great Sioux War.

John Pommer Grave.
Private John Pommer of Company I, Fifth Cavalry, died along French Creek on October 3, 1876, stricken not by combat wounds but chronic diarrhea. Crook's men spent nearly a month in the Black Hills recuperating from the rigors of the summer campaign, but Pommer's luck ran out.

5 GETTING THERE

Deadwood, South Dakota

The largest gold rush community in the Black Hills, Deadwood is approximately forty miles northwest of Rapid City on U.S. 385. Of all the communities in the area today, it is Deadwood that retains the strongest impressions of the gold rush era. Deadwood and nearby Lead offer interesting museums; the once longest continuously operating gold mine in the United States—the Homestake, chartered in 1876; and the grave of James B. "Wild Bill" Hickok, who was murdered in a Deadwood saloon on August 2, 1876.

TRAVELER'S TIP: Bear Butte [27] and Fort Meade [45] are nearby.

Wild Bill Hickok's Grave. *This well-cared-for grave in Deadwood's Mt. Moriah Cemetery recalls the fortune seekers populating the Black Hills boomtowns in 1876, while elsewhere on the northern plains Lakotas, Cheyennes, and soldiers contested possession of those goldfields and a way of life.*

CHAPER III
THE SUMMER WAR, MARCH–OCTOBER 1876

IN MID-1875 A GROUP OF Bozeman, Montana, businessmen embarked for the Yellowstone River to establish a trading post in Crow Indian country. Named Fort Pease [6] to honor partner Fellows David Pease, the small cottonwood outpost located in a broad bottom just below the mouth of the Bighorn River captured but a modest trade, mostly from independent white wolfers. Profits were marginal at the fort, mostly because of incessant predation by the Sioux, who laid siege to the post and its inhabitants throughout the winter. The fort was an easy target as it was located in prime buffalo hunting country favored by dissident bands of Lakota, led by Sitting Bull, Crazy Horse,

Montana Historical Society Photograph Archives

*James S. Brisbin.
Major Brisbin's brief sortie from Fort Ellis to the relief of Fort Pease in February and March 1876 was the army's initial movement against the Lakotas in the wake of their having been declared hostile by the government. To the tribesmen, the action may have portended an army onslaught that grew more fearsome with each passing season.*

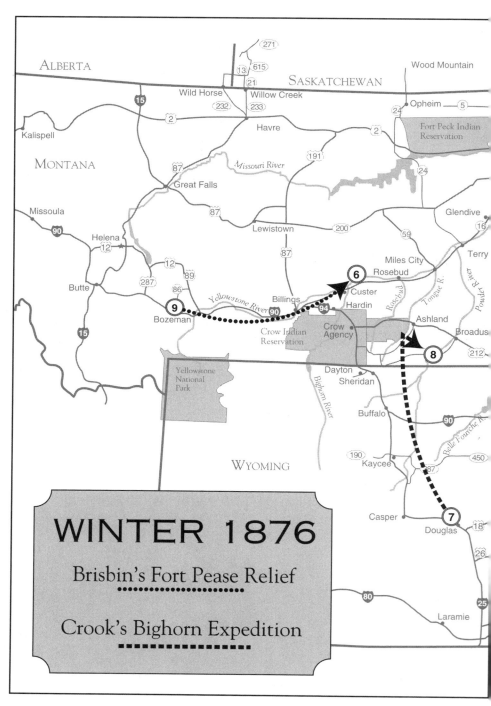

ALBERTA

SASKATCHEWAN

Wood Mountain

Wild Horse   Willow Creek

Opheim

Kalispell

MONTANA

Havre

Fort Peck Indian
Reservation

Missouri River

Great Falls

Lewistown

Glendive

Missoula

Helena

Miles City

Rosebud

Terry

Butte

Yellowstone River

Billings

Custer
Hardin

Ashland

Broadus

Bozeman

Crow Indian
Reservation

Crow
Agency

Yellowstone
National
Park

Dayton
Sheridan

Bighorn River

Buffalo

WYOMING

Kaycee

Casper

Douglas

Laramie

WINTER 1876

Brisbin's Fort Pease Relief
•••••••••••••••••••••••••

Crook's Bighorn Expedition
■ ■ ■ ■ ■ ■ ■ ■ ■ ■ ■ ■ ■ ■ ■

Courtesy of John Popovich

Fort Pease.
At the request of Charles Kessler of Helena, Paul McCormick
provided this 1919 historic sketch by V. R. Goode. McCormick
was a founder and occupant of the small trader's fort during its
brief existence in 1875 and 1876.

and others. These bands had become targets of the government's campaign to sweep the landscape of Indians in order to open the region to
Euramerican settlement.

The traders called on the army for help. Their pleas for relief were
finally heeded by General Alfred Terry in late February 1876, when he
ordered Major James S. Brisbin, Second Cavalry, and companies of cavalry and infantry from Fort Ellis [9] to their aid. The relief battalion reached
Fort Pease [6] on March 4, finding nineteen survivors; six men had been
killed and eight wounded during the siege. Brisbin did not engage the
Sioux, but evidence of their presence was everywhere. Having unwittingly
prefaced the Great Sioux War, the relief column returned to Fort Ellis in
mid-March in time to join Colonel John Gibbon's formal movement
against the Sioux.

6 GETTING THERE

Fort Pease, Montana

A small trading post in Crow Indian country, Fort Pease was besieged in the winter of 1876 by non-reservation Sioux, who killed six men and wounded eight others before government troops came to the aid of the traders. The site of Fort Pease was obliterated years ago by the meandering of the Yellowstone River, and no commemorative monument exists. The proximity is accessible, however, via Interstate 94 at Custer, Montana. From there take the unnumbered road exiting the town to the north. Soon after crossing the Yellowstone River the road forks. Take the right fork, generally following the river, to the Cunningham Ranch in the Pease Bottom, approximately nine and a half miles. The fort lay just beyond ranch headquarters. This is private property.

Army Camp at Fort Fetterman, 1877.

With Fort Fetterman faintly visible on the distant hilltop, the floodplain of the North Platte River is filled with men and matériel bound for Montana during a troop redeployment following the Great Sioux War. The scene is eerily similar to the seasons of campaigning in 1876. This photograph was taken by Private Charles Howard, Fourth Infantry.

Courtesy of Larry Ness

Fort Fetterman.
Museum exhibits in this original log officer quarters in part explore Fort Fetterman's role in the Great Sioux War. This was a desolate post and that quality is still evident at this remote Wyoming historic site.

SHERIDAN INTENDED A WINTER CAMPAIGN against the non-reservation Sioux while they were virtually immobilized in scattered winter camps, with the objective of disarming them and confining them to the Great Sioux Reservation in the Dakota Territory. Orders commencing the campaign generated a flurry of activity in western Montana, eastern Dakota, and southern Wyoming. General Crook was the first to take the field with a column of soldiers, marching forth from central Wyoming about the time Brisbin relieved Fort Pease [6]. Crook's column of nearly nine hundred men, dubbed the Big Horn Expedition, formed on the North Platte River at Fort Fetterman, Wyoming [7]. It was a small, unattractive post but ultimately among the most important of the Great Sioux War.

Fort Fetterman, Wyoming

GETTING THERE 7

Fort Fetterman functioned as Crook's staging base for three consecutive drives into the Powder River country. To visit the fort, travel Wyoming 93 7.7 miles north from Douglas, Wyoming, to the Fort Fetterman State Historic Site. The route is well signed. Two original buildings survive, one housing a small museum. Building foundations and the grounds are well marked.

Joseph J. Reynolds.
Bearing the grade of major general in this Civil War–era photograph, Reynolds's military career was doomed by his failings in the Powder River battle. The colonel was humiliated by a court-martial in January 1877, and he retired that summer.

AFTER ENDURING HARSH WINTER weather, Crook's column learned of an Indian encampment on the Powder River **[8]**, a short distance into Montana. Hoping to surprise and capture the village, Crook ordered the congenial, fifty-four-year-old Colonel Joseph J. Reynolds, Third Cavalry, with six companies of the Second and Third Cavalry, to close on the village. Reynolds struck the camp at dawn, March 17, and in a morning battle destroyed the tepees and captured eight hundred Indian ponies. When the Indians retaliated, however, the troops withdrew under sharp fire. Reynolds left his dead on the field and that night he lost the ponies. Crook was enraged when he learned of these events, and he initiated court-martial charges immediately. Most damaging for the U.S. Army, the village contained Northern Cheyenne Indians led by Old Bear, not Lakotas, and those tribesmen rallied quickly and participated in most subsequent phases of the Great Sioux War.

8 GETTING THERE **Powder River Battlefield, Montana**

Colonel Joseph Reynolds's unsuccessful attack on a village of previously neutral Northern Cheyennes in March 1876 brought the tribe into the war. The Powder River, or Reynolds, battlefield is located 35.8 miles southwest of Broadus, Montana, on the Moorhead road paralleling the Powder River. A large stone pyramid on the east side of the road marks the site. Embedded in the monument are government grave markers for the four soldiers killed in the battle. The Cheyenne village was located in the river bottom east of the monument. This is private property.

Powder River Battlefield.
The fighting between companies of the Second and Third Cavalry and an encampment of Northern Cheyennes on March 17, 1876, occurred partly in the timbered bottoms of the Powder and partly on the bench and highlands beyond. The battle monument is located on the distant bench.

Powder River Battlefield Monument.
This unique rock pyramid has imbedded in it four vintage government grave markers commemorating the Second and Third Cavalrymen killed in the March 17 clash.

WHILE GENERAL CROOK REORGANIZED, Colonel John Gibbon advanced his Montana Column east from Fort Ellis [9]. To create this force of 450 infantry and cavalry, the smallest of the initial field commands engaged in the Sioux War, Gibbon nearly depleted the scattered meager posts of western Montana. Of the various military garrisons in Gibbon's administrative control, thereafter only Fort Ellis [9] played a visible role in the war as a modest supply and consolidation site. Gibbon took to the trail on March 30, joining General Terry's column on the Yellowstone six weeks later.

9 GETTING THERE

Fort Ellis, Montana

Fort Ellis, which acted as a supply and consolidation site during the war, stood one mile northeast of Bozeman on Montana 86. Nothing survives of the fort, but a small monument located along the highway marks the site.

Fort Hartsuff.
This small, one-company outpost was established in 1874 and abandoned in 1881 following the advent of Fort Niobrara. Most buildings seen here survive.

Nebraska State Historical Society

Alfred Terry.
Much of the Great Sioux War
occurred in Terry's Department of
Dakota. During the summer of 1876
Terry was the senior-most officer
engaged in the field.

State Historical Society of North Dakota

INDEPENDENT OF THE GENERAL
ORCHESTRATIONS of the war, a
small band of Sioux warriors embarked
on a raiding expedition in central Ne-
braska. On April 28 the warriors clashed with a detachment of mounted
Twenty-third Infantrymen led by Second Lieutenant Charles H. Heyl dispatched from nearby Fort Hartsuff [10]. In the so-called "Battle of the
Blowout" occurring on Grace, or Gracie, Creek, a dozen miles north of
the fort, an Indian and a U.S. soldier were killed in sharp fighting. But for
this brief, dramatic clash, Fort Hartsuff's role in the Great Sioux War was
minimal.

GETTING THERE 10

Fort Hartsuff and
Grace Creek Skirmish, Nebraska

Stemming an Indian raid into central Nebraska, troops from Fort
Hartsuff clashed with a band of Sioux warriors in April 1876. To get to
the fort, from Ord take Nebraska 11 six miles northwest and turn east
at the village of Elyria. Follow the paved, unnumbered road four miles
to the well-marked entrance to Fort Hartsuff State Historical Park.
Fort Hartsuff is intact, surviving as perhaps the finest example of a
small, plains-style fort in the United States. The Grace Creek skirmish site is not marked and is virtually inaccessible. Inquiry at Fort
Hartsuff is essential for a visit. The skirmish site is private property.

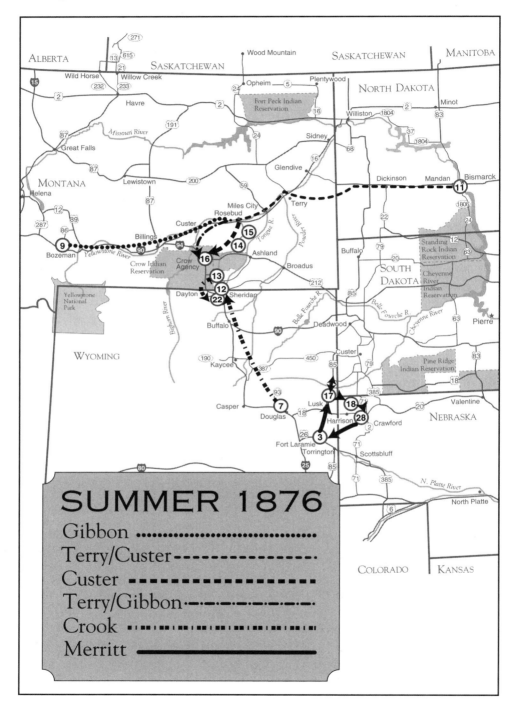

SHERIDAN'S HOPES FOR A SUCCESSFUL winter campaign against the Sioux were foiled by the harsh springtime weather and Reynolds's mismanagement of the opening action. Meanwhile, General Terry's 925-man Dakota Column of cavalry and infantry finally took the field on May 17, having been organized at Fort Abraham Lincoln [11], southwest of Bismarck. The Northern Pacific Railroad had reached Bismarck in 1873, and the city, fort, and associated Camp Hancock were already well-established forward stations supporting military operations in Indian country.

As in Gibbon's circumstance in Montana, the Dakota Column was composed of troops drawn from posts scattered across the Dakota frontier. Most visible in Terry's force were the twelve companies of the Seventh Cavalry under its mercurial junior commander, Lieutenant Colonel George A. Custer. According to earlier planning, Custer was to have commanded the Dakota Column, but he had recently incurred President Grant's wrath and now marched subordinate to Terry.

GETTING THERE 11

Fort Abraham Lincoln, North Dakota

Fort Abraham Lincoln State Park is located four miles south of Mandan on North Dakota 1806. General Terry's Dakota Column organized here before taking the field on May 17, 1876; a month and a half later, wounded soldiers from the Little Bighorn battle [16] were returned here for treatment. Five buildings at the cavalry post, including Custer's home and a barrack, have been reconstructed. A fine museum provides an orientation to the site, and foundations, markers, and monuments abound, including at the Fort McKeen infantry post on the hill overlooking the Missouri River and cavalry square.

TRAVELER'S TIP: Fort Yates and the Standing Rock Reservation [43] are nearby.

AS GIBBON'S FORCE GAINED THE MIDDLE Yellowstone River and Terry's Dakota Column launched westward, a third force in Sheridan's scheme of encirclement took the field in Wyoming. Again led by General Crook and this time dubbed the Big Horn and Yellowstone Expedition, twenty fresh infantry and cavalry companies drawn from the Department of the Platte marched northward from Fort Fetterman [7]

Custer House, Fort Abraham Lincoln.
This meticulous reconstruction and refurnishing of Custer's quarters at Fort Abraham Lincoln dates from the late 1980s. When linked with the Sioux and Northern Cheyenne village site and adjacent battlefield at the Little Bighorn in Montana, a paradoxical view of military and Indian life emerges.

Tongue River Heights Skirmish.
This woodcut of the June 9, 1876, skirmish appeared in the September 1890 issue of Frank Leslie's Popular Monthly.

Courtesy of Jerome A. Greene

with a renewed confidence and desire to defeat the Sioux. After establishing a base camp on Goose Creek in northern Wyoming, Crook's 1,100-man force ambled onto the Tongue River on June 7. In an audacious move two days later, several hundred Sioux and Cheyenne warriors appeared on the bluffs overlooking Crook's camp and fired into the tentage [12]. The shooting was at extreme distances and more annoying than harmful, but Crook finally ordered one of his cavalry battalions to drive away the attackers. The Indians quickly fled, and two were reported killed. Three army horses and one mule were killed.

GETTING THERE 12

Tongue River Heights Skirmish, Wyoming

The Tongue River Heights skirmish site is not marked. To visit the area where Crook encountered Sioux and Cheyenne warriors on June 9, 1876, travel Wyoming 336 east from Sheridan. In about three miles the valley of Prairie Dog Creek opens on the left, as does a gravel road following the creek northward to its junction with the Tongue River. Crook's camp and the site of the skirmish are located where the creek and river join, about ten miles north. This is private property.

TRAVELER'S TIP: The Rosebud battlefield [13] and Crook's Camp Cloud Peak [22] are nearby.

George Crook.
This photograph of the Department of the Platte commander was taken in January 1877 by D. S. Mitchell of Cheyenne, Wyoming. By then the Sioux War fighting was over for Crook, though there were numerous uncertainties at the agencies and in the Yellowstone River country.

Rosebud Battlefield.
This panoramic view from General Crook's field headquarters overlooks the Rosebud battlefield. The site is vast and pristine and perhaps the finest extant example of a preserved Great Sioux War battlefield. Some five thousand acres comprising most of the Rosebud battlefield were acquired by the State of Montana in the 1970s, preserving the heritage of the battle and the diligent efforts of Slim Kobold, longtime battlefield owner, who devoted himself to saving the site.

UNDAUNTED BY THE SIOUX, Crook's force crossed the Tongue and moved onto Rosebud Creek. As the expedition rested and prepared coffee on the morning of June 17 the Indians struck suddenly and in force [13]. For six hours, Sioux and Cheyenne warriors led by Crazy Horse parried with Crook's troops on a battlefield that eventually spanned five miles of creek bottom and heights. Believing his attackers' village was nearby, Crook dispatched portions of his cavalry to assault their camp. He expected to support his cavalry just as quickly as he could disengage from the morning field, but the warriors could not be beaten away. Ultimately fearing for the safety of his divided command, Crook ordered his cavalry's return. Back trailing to the battlefield by a different route, the cavalry arrived, opportunely, behind the Indians. When attacked from the rear, the warriors quit the fight.

Crook held the field and proclaimed a victory. Crazy Horse later estimated Indian casualties at thirty-nine killed and sixty-three wounded. The troops tallied ten killed and twenty-one wounded. Crook knew that a major Indian village was near and had he advanced against it, it probably would have scattered. But timidity overcame him. His command had expended twenty-five thousand rounds of ammunition at the Rosebud [13], and he professed an inordinate concern for his wounded. By retiring to Goose Creek, Crook quashed any prospects of a meaningful victory. And instead of the Indian encampment scattering, it grew stronger each passing day, perhaps doubling or tripling in size by the time Custer encountered it eight days later.

Rosebud Battlefield, Montana   GETTING THERE 13

Crazy Horse attacked Crook's encampment on grounds now known as the Rosebud Battlefield State Monument. Their battle raged for six hours, leaving thirty-nine Indians and ten U.S. soldiers dead. The battlefield is located twenty-four miles south of Busby on Montana 314, and one mile west of the highway. An aged stone monument overlooks the intersection, and other signs direct the way. Like many remote Sioux War fields, the site is pristine. The state has erected several interpretive markers at the entrance to the field, and other vintage monuments are scattered about. A primitive road loops through a corner of the site, but most primary locations are better accessed by foot. Crook's field headquarters stood on the high ridge to the west. The battlefield encompasses public and private land.

TRAVELER'S TIP: The Tongue River Heights skirmish site [12] and the Northern Cheyenne Reservation [48] are nearby.

AFTER STRUGGLING ACROSS THE NORTH DAKOTA badlands and enduring a fierce springtime blizzard on June 1, Terry's Dakota Column reached the Yellowstone River on the eleventh. Colonel Gibbon had advanced ahead of his column to confer with Terry, but he bore no useful intelligence on the whereabouts of the Sioux, whose main camps were still believed to be on one of the principal tributaries of the Yellowstone.

George A. Custer.
More than any other warrior of 1876–77, Custer epitomizes the enduring intrigue of the Great Sioux War. Neither hero nor fool, Custer was a capable officer and his regiment was perhaps the finest the army deployed in 1876. His spectacular defeat at the Little Bighorn by warriors fighting for home and kin glorifies antagonist and protagonist alike.

Montana Historical Society Photograph Archives

Meanwhile, on June 10 Terry ordered Major Marcus A. Reno and six companies of the Seventh Cavalry to scout the valleys of the Powder and Tongue rivers. Neither watercourse subsequently yielded useful information, but Mitch Boyer, Reno's mixed-blood scout lent from Gibbon's command, urged a reconnaissance of the middle Rosebud valley. There Reno

State Historical Society of North Dakota

Marcus Reno.
Reno's debatable conduct on the scout preceding the Little Bighorn fight and during that engagement were stigmas he never overcame. His career quickly shattered, and he was dismissed from the service in 1880. Ironically, in 1967 Reno's remains were reinterred in the Custer National Cemetery.

State Historical Society of North Dakota

Sitting Bull.
This well-known photograph of Sitting Bull was taken about 1884 by the Bismarck photographer David F. Barry.

found numerous fresh signs, including many campsites and broad Indian trails heading upstream. In scouting the Rosebud, Reno had advanced beyond the authority of his orders, yet he had finally found the evidence that Terry and Gibbon sought. Reno countermarched to the mouth of the Rosebud and conferred with Gibbon on June 18. Terry, meanwhile, awaited at the mouth of the Tongue, where Reno was to have concluded his reconnaissance.

Reno and Custer reunited on June 20 midway between the Rosebud and Tongue and marched for the Rosebud, reaching there at midday on the twenty-first. Terry arrived shortly aboard the steamboat *Far West*, one of several boats supporting troop movements on the Yellowstone. The field commanders conferred aboard the *Far West* that afternoon. Terry ordered Custer and all twelve companies of the Seventh to follow the great Indian trail up Rosebud Creek toward the valley of the Little Bighorn River. Terry and Gibbon, meanwhile, would travel the Yellowstone to the mouth of the Bighorn River, and up the Bighorn to the Little Bighorn, trapping any fleeing Indians there. Terry reasoned that he would be at the mouth of the Little Bighorn by June 26.

With a great deal of pomp, Custer's cavalry departed the Yellowstone on June 22 and for the next two days examined numerous large and small Indian village sites, including a great sun dance camp where the Hunkpapa Sioux leader Sitting Bull, as the world learned later, experienced his prophetic vision of soldiers falling upside down into his village [14]. Beyond the sun dance camp, the Indian trail grew fresher and broader and turned west from the Rosebud.

14 GETTING THERE

Sitting Bull's Sun Dance Camp, Montana

Sitting Bull interpreted his sun dance vision of soldiers falling upside down into his village to mean that a great victory was imminent. The battle of the Little Bighorn occurred two weeks later.

The great Sioux sun dance camp is five and a half miles north of Lame Deer on Montana 39. The valley floor along Rosebud Creek is narrow here, and the surrounding highlands are dramatic. The camp site was extensive and stretched for perhaps a mile. This is federal and private property.

TRAVELER'S TIP: Custer's trail to the Little Bighorn [15], the Lame Deer battlefield [37], and the Northern Cheyenne Reservation [48] are nearby.

Custer's June 22 Campsite.
This marker along Rosebud Creek commemorates the Seventh Cavalry's first night camp after departing General Terry and the Yellowstone River.

Custer's June 23 Campsite.
This small scoria marker commemorates the Seventh
Cavalry's second campsite on Rosebud Creek, en route to
the Little Bighorn.

A NIGHT MARCH TOOK CUSTER'S TROOPS to the divide between the Rosebud and Little Bighorn, and in the early morning light Custer's scouts pointed to evidence of a large Indian village in the distant valley. That was exactly the news Custer sought. He had intended to rest his command on the twenty-fifth and position it after nightfall for a dawn attack on June 26. Small parties of Indians were occasionally seen, however, threading their way to the Little Bighorn. Custer fretted that these tribesmen might discover his command and that the discovery would disperse the distant village. As well, Custer learned that a small party of Indians had been discovered on his back trail and that shots were exchanged. That news intensified his urgency. In fact, these were Cheyennes fresh from the Red Cloud Agency [28], following the large trail just as the soldiers were. Custer could not have known that, of course, and, convinced that he was discovered, pressed an attack on the afternoon of June 25.

Montana Historical Society Museum

Reno's Retreat.
This 1961 pen and ink sketch by the Montana artist J. K. Ralston captures a sense of the pandemonium enveloping Reno's withdrawal from his timber position in the Little Bighorn valley to the bluffs across the river.

15 GETTING THERE

Custer's Trail to the Little Bighorn, Montana

To follow Custer's trail along Rosebud Creek to the site of the most famous battle of the Great Sioux War, exit Interstate 94 on Rosebud Creek Road, following Rosebud County 447 south to its intersection with Montana 39. Continue south to Lame Deer and turn west on U.S. 212 to Busby. Thereafter, Custer's route to the Little Bighorn is inaccessible by automobile but is south of and roughly parallel to U.S. 212. The Nathan Short marker [23] is at 6.7 miles. Custer's June 22 campsite marker is at 10.4 miles. Custer's June 23 campsite marker is at 43.4 miles. Sitting Bull's sun dance camp [14] is at 52.6 miles. These sites are private property.

TRAVELER'S TIP: The Lame Deer battlefield [37] is nearby.

AS CUSTER DESCENDED RENO CREEK, he divided his regiment into battalions, with Captain Frederick W. Benteen and three companies ordered to scout in a southwesterly direction and block any flight up the Little Bighorn; Reno and three companies to strike the village at its upper end; and Custer reserving five companies to strike the village at its middle or lower end. Captain Thomas M. McDougall trailed with one company and the pack train.

Reno engaged first, leading his companies into the upper end of an extraordinarily large Indian encampment whose warriors enveloped him effortlessly. Unable to hold his initial position at the periphery of the village, Reno withdrew to a dense stand of timber along the river. Indian pressure made that stand equally untenable, and the major soon lost all composure and led a pell-mell retreat to the high bluffs east of the river.

Little Bighorn Battlefield.
Like the Rosebud, the Little Bighorn battlefield is a vast landscape spanning some six miles from south to north. This vista from Custer Hill overlooks Deep Ravine and the valley that the Lakota and Cheyenne encampment filled for more than two miles.

Little Bighorn Battlefield Visitor Center.
Though typically crowded with visitors, the National Park Service's visitor facilities at Little Bighorn provide a rounded introduction to the Great Sioux War and the intriguing battle occurring there on June 25–26, 1876. This view from Custer Hill overlooks the park visitor center and Custer National Cemetery in the trees.

Custer, meanwhile, advanced up the east side of the Little Bighorn to Medicine Tail coulee and deployed his companies into battle. Ever after, battle scholars have speculated on Custer's precise movements. Perhaps they were mostly defensive as the Lakota and Cheyenne warriors appeared after repulsing Reno to engulf Custer's command. Perhaps he and several companies moved aggressively down Medicine Tail Coulee to strike the village, until driven back up Deep Coulee, with remnants of the command finally uniting along Custer Hill for something of a last stand. However Custer's portion of the June 25 battle [16] unfolded, the fighting seems to have been quick and conclusive.

Reno and most of his command survived, entrenched on the bluffs high above the Little Bighorn five miles south of Custer's position. There he was joined by Benteen's battalion and McDougall's pack train, and

Courtesy of Jerome A. Greene

Custer Hill Monuments.

This photograph from the 1890s shows the culmination of several different monumenting efforts at the then–Custer Battlefield National Cemetery. The granite obelisk crowning Custer Hill rose in mid-1881 commemorating the battle and the mass reburial of Seventh Cavalry enlisted casualties. Individual marble markers were placed across the field in 1890 to denote the original scattered interments. These visitors, including two soldiers on the right, were probably from nearby Fort Custer. The man at center stands at Custer's marker.

they resisted fiery attacks through virtually all of June 26. The great village, however, dispersed just before Gibbon and Terry advanced onto the field, having traveled overland from the mouth of the Bighorn. On the morning of June 27, Gibbon's scouts discovered the mutilated remains of Custer's dead and the scattered debris of the Indian encampment. The soldiers spent June 28 burying 263 dead and preparing Reno's wounded for evacuation. That day Captain Edward Ball reconnoitered south with his Second Cavalry company and found where the great Indian trail divided, some components turning southeast and others southwest, while burning the prairie behind them. The greatest Indian battle in the American West had ended.

Courtesy of James Brust

The Place Where Custer Fell.
*This 1877 stereographic image by John H. Fouch is the
earliest known photograph of the Little Bighorn battlefield.
Horse bones and battle debris still littered the field, though
Lieutenant Colonel Michael Sheridan's reburial party had
recently finished policing the battleground. The army's large
granite monument erected in 1881 was placed on this spot.*

GETTING
THERE **16**

Little Bighorn Battlefield, Montana

The site where Sioux and Cheyenne warriors defeated Custer and the Seventh Cavalry is the most famous battlefield of the Great Sioux War, and of any American Indian war. To visit the Little Bighorn Battlefield National Monument, go one mile south of Crow Agency on Interstate 90, and one mile east on U.S. 212. A National Park Service visitor center provides an overview of the battle and displays significant Indian and soldier artifacts. Army grave markers dot the field showing where the bodies of Seventh Cavalrymen were found and first buried. The individual interments were later consolidated into a mass grave atop Custer Hill, which in 1881 was further memorialized with the erection of a large granite obelisk. The adjoining Custer National Cemetery holds the graves of Major Reno and other Seventh Cavalrymen associated with the battle.

A park road connects the visitor center area with the Reno-Benteen entrenchment site, five miles south. At that point a self-guided walking tour explains the later phases of the battle.

The great Indian encampment stretched along the Little Bighorn River roughly parallel to and east of present Interstate 90 from the U.S. 212 interchange south to the Garryowen interchange. Several commemorative markers are located in the village site and Reno's valley positions. Directions to these monuments can be obtained at the Little Bighorn Battlefield visitor center.

This battlefield is vast and encompasses federal land in National Park Service and Bureau of Indian Affairs jurisdiction, plus numerous private holdings.

TRAVELER'S TIP: The Fort Custer site [39] is nearby.

ON JUNE 30 THE RENO-BENTEEN WOUNDED were placed aboard the steamer *Far West* and delivered down the Yellowstone and Missouri rivers to medical attention at Fort Abraham Lincoln [11]. The merciful river passage of approximately nine hundred miles was completed in a record-setting pace of fifty-four hours. Other survivors of the Little Bighorn battle encamped with Terry and Gibbon in the Pease Bottom along the Yellowstone to ponder the uncertainties of this disastrous Indian war.

While the field commanders lay stymied, General Sheridan expedited matters from his headquarters in Chicago. He first dealt with the explosive surge of Black Hills–bound miners traveling, often at considerable peril, from Cheyenne to Fort Laramie [3] and on to Custer City [4] and Deadwood [5]. This Black Hills road crossed the broad and well-worn Powder River trail connecting the northern camps and the Nebraska agencies. Indians were encountered frequently enough in May and June to warrant deploying the Fifth Cavalry from the Department of the Missouri to safeguard the road. The Fifth used Fort Laramie [3] as its supply base, reaffirming a supporting role perfected by that post during Sheridan's and Crook's successive movements against the Sioux.

Sheridan also ordered the establishment of two single-company infantry outposts on the trail beyond Fort Laramie [3]. Camp on Sage Creek, Wyoming [17], and Camp Mouth of Red Canyon, Dakota [20], bolstered the army's presence on the Black Hills road. The Fifth Cavalry served as the mobile force linking Fort Laramie and these infantry subposts.

Reno-Benteen Monument.
This solitary granite monument was dedicated in 1929 to commemorate the defensive position occupied by Seventh Cavalrymen from the evening of June 25 until their relief by Terry's and Gibbon's command two days later. The site is five miles south of Custer Hill on the Little Bighorn battlefield.

Steamboat *Far West*.
Captained by perhaps the greatest of the Missouri River steamboatmen, Grant Marsh, the Far West *played a key role in the summer campaign against the Sioux, both as a supply and ferry boat and as a vessel of mercy transporting U.S. wounded from the Little Bighorn to medical care at Fort Abraham Lincoln. Photograph by F. Jay Haynes, 1880.*

Beyond providing a reassuring presence to Black Hills–bound prospectors, the soldiers at Sage Creek also played a minor role in the Fifth Cavalry's forced march to Warbonnet Creek, Nebraska [18], in mid-July, to intercept a large band of Cheyenne Indians bound from the Red Cloud Agency [28] to the northern camps. The army rightly believed that these Cheyennes would strengthen the Lakota resistance and had to be stopped.

Hat Creek Stage Station, near Camp on Sage Creek.
The Hat Creek Stage Station seen here dates to the 1880s,
a relic of the continued use of this site by soldiers and
the Cheyenne and Black Hills Stage, Mail and Express
Company. Today this is the last surviving stage station on the
epic Black Hills Road.

GETTING THERE **17**

Camp on Sage Creek, Wyoming

Sheridan ordered the establishment of a single-company infantry outpost on Sage Creek to protect gold seekers traveling the Black Hills Road. Camp on Sage Creek and the adjacent Hat Creek Stage Station are 13.3 miles north of Lusk on U.S. 85. At the "Fort Hat Creek" interpretive sign on the east side of the highway, travel east one mile to a country school, then south one mile to the Hat Creek station. The building is an original 1880s log station from the Cheyenne-Deadwood stage. The army camp was on the east side of Sage Creek opposite the stage station. This is private property.

These sites are, indeed, on Sage Creek. The references to Hat Creek are historical but erroneous.

Little Bighorn Battlefield National Monument

Wesley Merritt.
Colonel of the Fifth Cavalry, Merritt's prompt response in the Warbonnet Creek affair provided the army's first success in the Great Sioux War.

NEWS OF THE CHEYENNE FLIGHT from the Red Cloud Agency [28] had come to Fort Laramie [3] on July 11 from Camp Robinson and was received on the thirteenth by Colonel Wesley Merritt, commanding the Fifth Cavalry. Merritt was then en route to General Crook, Merritt's troops soon to be replaced on the Black Hills trail by Fourth Cavalrymen. Merritt fully understood the urgency posed by the Cheyenne flight and halted his travel just north of Fort Laramie. After back trailing to the Sage Creek army camp [17] and collecting the resident Twenty-third Infantry company as a wagon guard, he continued east to Warbonnet Creek [18], confident of intercepting the fleeing Cheyennes.

At dawn on July 17, an advance party from the Cheyenne band ran headlong into the Fifth Cavalry and were turned back to the Red Cloud Agency [28]. Shots were exchanged, but the lone casualty was a Cheyenne warrior named Yellow Hair, who was killed and scalped by the Fifth's scout and erstwhile showman, William F. "Buffalo Bill" Cody. As the troops rushed by, Cody waved Yellow Hair's braid aloft proclaiming it the "first scalp for Custer."

Warbonnet Creek Skirmish Site.
The Warbonnet Creek skirmish of July 17 occurred on this rolling Nebraska prairie. The distant hillocks were used as observation positions by men of the Fifth Cavalry.

GETTING THERE

18

Warbonnet Creek Skirmish, Nebraska

Colonel Wesley Merritt and the Fifth Cavalry intercepted a band of Cheyennes fleeing the Red Cloud Agency [28] at Warbonnet Creek. The skirmish site is north of present-day Harrison. To get to the site, take the unnumbered county road north from the center of town for approximately sixteen miles, always maintaining a northerly bearing at several forks in the road. At sixteen miles watch for the Montrose sign; turn right, and continue east for another eight miles to that now-abandoned townsite, identified by a small Catholic church on a hill. The skirmish monument is visible three hundred yards north of the church. A Cody–Yellow Hair fight monument, commemorating the place where "Buffalo Bill" claimed the infamous "first scalp for Custer," is a hundred and fifty yards northeast of the church. This is federal land.

TRAVELER'S TIP: Camp Robinson and the Red Cloud Agency [28] are nearby.

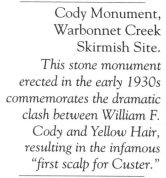

Cody Monument,
Warbonnet Creek
Skirmish Site.
*This stone monument
erected in the early 1930s
commemorates the dramatic
clash between William F.
Cody and Yellow Hair,
resulting in the infamous
"first scalp for Custer."*

THE WARBONNET EPISODE [18] CONCLUDED at Camp Robinson
and the Red Cloud Agency [28] on the evening of July 17, the Indians
and troops arriving a short while apart. Though Red Cloud and Spotted
Tail both counseled peace to their young warriors and these Cheyennes,
their words were not binding and the Nebraska agencies were a continuing source of fighting men and weaponry throughout the conflict. Though
the focus of the Great Sioux War would return to this post and agency
along Nebraska's White River, Merritt's Fifth Cavalry tarried there only
briefly before resuming the march to Fort Laramie [3] and General Crook.

Meanwhile, in early July Crook dispatched Second Lieutenant Frederick W. Sibley, Second Cavalry, with two dozen men and
scouts, to explore northwestward for the Sioux. Following the old Bozeman
Trail [2], the party reached the valley of the Little Bighorn River on the
morning of July 7, where they encountered bands of Lakota and Cheyenne warriors in tempered flight from the Little Bighorn battlefield [16].
The Indians as quickly discovered Sibley's men and engaged the soldiers
in a running fight up the Little Bighorn and into the mountains [19]. The
fray intensified until the soldiers finally eluded their pursuers by climbing
deeper and higher into the Bighorns. On July 9 they reached Crook's camp
bearing news that the Tongue and Little Bighorn river country was alive
with Indians.

Sibley Scout Monument. *This marker high in the Bighorn Mountains commemorates Frederick Sibley's running fight with Lakota and Cheyenne Indians in early July 1876. If anything, the episode verified the Indians' continuing prowess in the wake of the Rosebud and Little Bighorn battles.*

19 GETTING THERE

Sibley Scout, Wyoming

On July 7, Lakota and Cheyenne warriors, fresh from the Little Bighorn fight, encountered Second Lieutenant Sibley and his men, who were scouting the area on General Crook's orders. The Indians chased Sibley deep into the Bighorn Mountains. Cheyenne chief White Antelope was killed in the fray.

The first half of the Sibley scout can be followed by traveling Interstate 90 north from Sheridan, and U.S. 14 west to Dayton, which roughly parallels the Bozeman Trail [2]. Thereafter the route of the scout is uncharted in mountainous terrain. A monument to the affair is located high in the Bighorn Mountains. Continue west of Dayton on U.S. 14 for twenty-two miles to the Forest Service campground and picnic area at Sibley Lake. The monument is in the picnic area at the foot of the Sibley Lake dam. This is federal property.

OTHER SMALL CLASHES OCCURRED during the summer, several in the vicinity of the Powder River trail. On August 1 the infantry company garrisoning the Red Canyon camp [20] in the southwestern Black Hills responded to gunshots at a nearby ranch along the Cheyenne River, where they engaged Indians in a lively nighttime fight. One warrior was killed and several "American" horses were lost. On August 2 thirty Indians attacked the "Heck" Reel supply train bound from Cheyenne to Fort Fetterman [7]. The wagon boss and a teamster were killed and three wagons burned before the attackers withdrew.

GETTING THERE (20)

Camp Mouth of Red Canyon, South Dakota

One of two single-company camps established by General Sheridan in the summer of 1876 to guard prospectors traveling along the Black Hills Road, the army camp at Red Canyon, often mistakenly called Camp Collier, is located 3.5 miles east of Edgemont, South Dakota, where U.S. 18 makes a pronounced climb into the Black Hills. The site is just north of the highway at the mouth of Red Canyon. This is private property.

Camp Mouth of Red Canyon.
Scattered surface undulations mark the army's Camp Mouth of Red Canyon. The site was aptly named, with the picturesque Red Canyon opening immediately and prominently north of the site.

ALONG THE YELLOWSTONE, the Lakotas and Cheyennes were equally emboldened by their successes over Crook and Custer. Earlier that summer Terry had established a supply depot at the mouth of the Powder River [21], one of several on the Yellowstone. A small Sixth and Seventeenth Infantry complement commanded by Major Orlando H. Moore, Sixth Infantry, came under attack at the freshly abandoned Powder River Depot on August 2 as they loaded remaining supplies. Moore employed a twelve pounder Ordnance Rifle to drive off his attackers but sustained one casualty in the hurried fight.

21 GETTING THERE
Powder River Depot, Montana

The Powder River Depot was one of several supply camps established by General Terry along the Yellowstone. The site is located just east of the Powder's confluence with the Yellowstone. To visit the depot, exit Interstate 94 on the Powder River Road. Travel north to the frontage road, old U.S. 10, and continue east across the old Powder River highway bridge. Immediately east of the river turn north and pass under the east abutment of the Powder River railroad bridge. Rise to the bench above the river and follow either of two dirt traces to their end at the depot site, 1.5 miles northeast. Marking the site are monuments to scout Wesley Brockmeyer, killed in the August 2 fight, and to Seventh Cavalry Private William George, who died on the *Far West* of his Little Bighorn battle wounds and was interred at the depot. Sheridan Butte is the prominent landmark north of the Yellowstone. This is federal property.

TRAVELER'S TIP: The Cedar Creek battlefield [33] is nearby.

AFTER HIS BATTLE AT ROSEBUD CREEK [13] on June 17, General Crook spent the remainder of June and all of July camped along Goose Creek [22] reinforcing the Big Horn and Yellowstone Expedition. Immediately after the battle, Crook had evacuated his battle wounded and was subsequently criticized for not moving aggressively against the Indians. A comment by Crook in a letter to Sheridan, "I am at a loss what to do," expressed the malaise paralyzing the field commanders in the wake of the season's great Indian battles. The tribesmen were surprising aggressors at Rosebud and superb defensemen at Little Bighorn [16], and neither trait was expected.

William George Grave, Powder River Depot.
Two government grave markers, including this one for
Private William George of the Seventh Cavalry, denote the
site of General Terry's Powder River Depot. This briefly
used supply station along the Yellowstone River played a key
role in the summer campaign.

GETTING THERE **22**

Camp Cloud Peak, Wyoming

An interpretive marker near downtown Sheridan commemorates Crook's six-week sojourn along Goose Creek, where he and his troops recuperated after the battle at Rosebud [13] and awaited reinforcements. From Main Street take Dow two blocks west to a small park at the intersection of Dow and Alger streets. In actuality, Crook moved his camp repeatedly along the creek in this vicinity as he sought fresh grazing for the expedition's livestock.

TRAVELER'S TIP: The Bozeman Trail [2] and the Tongue River Heights skirmish site [12] are nearby.

FALL 1876

Crook's Late Summer Movement and Starvation March
•••••••••••••••••••••••••••••••••••

Crook's Powder River Expedition
━ ━ ━ ━ ━ ━ ━ ━ ━ ━ ━

Miles's Cedar Creek Expedition
━━━━━━━━━━━━━━━━━━

AS THE SUMMER WANED, reinforcements reached both Crook's and Terry's camps. Much bolstered and after finally communicating with each other directly rather than via a tortured Chicago route, the two generals met on August 10 along Rosebud Creek. While traveling the creek, men of Terry's and Crook's commands chanced upon the scattered remains of a soldier and his mount that were immediately identified as a trooper of C Company, Seventh Cavalry. By his company property number the soldier was subsequently identified as Private Nathan Short, a courier dispatched from Custer, perhaps bound to Terry, who escaped one fate only to meet another along Rosebud Creek.

GETTING THERE **23**

Nathan Short Marker on Rosebud Creek, Montana

A marker erected in 1983 commemorates Private Nathan Short of the Seventh Cavalry, who died purportedly carrying a message from Custer, perhaps to General Terry, during the Battle of the Little Bighorn. Exit Interstate 94 on the Rosebud Creek Road, traveling Rosebud County 447 south 6.7 miles to the site. This is private property.

TRAVELER'S TIP: A marker designating Custer's June 22 campsite [15] is nearby.

Nathan Short Marker. In 1886 local authorities reported the rediscovery and burial of the remains of Nathan Short of the Seventh Cavalry near this marker along Rosebud Creek.

THE COMBINED TERRY-CROOK FORCE marched together south of the Yellowstone for two weeks, but the enlarged command had lost its mobility and resolve. On August 25 the forces parted, Crook cutting eastward following a faint Indian trail and Terry remaining on the Yellowstone ostensibly to block any Indian movement across the river.

On September 6, General Terry quit the campaign. After pausing at Fort Buford [53] to investigate Indian crossings of the Missouri, on the seventeenth he boarded the steamer *Chambers* bound for Bismarck. In due course, Terry's troops commenced overland marches to their respective stations. Terry left behind the Fifth Infantry, commanded by Colonel Nelson A. Miles, and portions of the Twenty-second Infantry, commanded by Lieutenant Colonel Elwell S. Otis, with orders to entrench on the Yellowstone and continue the campaign. The Fifth Infantrymen erected a ramshackle log outpost on the west bank of the Tongue. Named Tongue River Cantonment [24], it was from there that Miles engaged in a tireless winter campaign that ultimately ended the fighting.

24 GETTING THERE

Tongue River Cantonment, Montana

Colonel Nelson Miles and the Fifth Infantry conducted winter operations from the Tongue River Cantonment. Nothing survives of the outpost, though its site is on private property immediately behind the Range Rider Museum on the west side of Miles City.

TRAVELER'S TIP: Fort Keogh [38] is nearby.

CROOK'S TROOPS, MEANWHILE, ambled eastward into Dakota Territory, and at the head of the Heart River the general made a fateful decision to cut for the Black Hills, seven or eight days' march to the south. Fort Abraham Lincoln [11] was a two- or three-day march to the east, and Crook's command was dangerously underprovisioned. The prospect of locating Indians tipped his decision, however, and Crook decreed that when necessary his men would eat horseflesh. On September 6 the Big Horn and Yellowstone Expedition commenced its fateful southbound journey.

Eager to obtain provisions from the Black Hills mining camps, on the evening of September 7 Crook forwarded a hundred and fifty carefully chosen men led by Captain Anson Mills, Third Cavalry, and

Tongue River Cantonment.
This photograph by John Fouch shows the Tongue River Cantonment in the winter of 1876–77. Crudely fabricated of cottonwood logs and with dirt roofs, the cantonment was no showplace. In mid-1877 the camp was succeeded by the formally appointed Fort Keogh.

First Lieutenant John W. Bubb, the expedition's commissary officer. When barely a day's ride ahead of the main column, Mills and Bubb chanced upon an Indian camp nestled in the Slim Buttes [25] belonging to the Minneconjou Sioux American Horse. Mills attacked the village at dawn on September 9.

The battle of Slim Buttes [25] continued throughout the ninth. A messenger to Crook brought the entire command to the site just before noon. By then the Indians held the high ground west of their village and rained an abusive fire upon the soldiers. Crook's troops scattered the warriors several different times that afternoon while they methodically destroyed the tepees. The villagers were well provisioned and the troops ate ravenously. Doubtless the discovery of numerous Custer battle [16] relics helped justify the attack. The soldiers were probably oblivious to the fact that the village was located on the Great Sioux Reservation.

Sioux Tepee and Seventh Cavalry Guidon.
Anson Mills collected and retained these and other Slim Buttes battle trophies. Today the buffalo skin tepee is in the collections of the Smithsonian Institution, while the guidon reposes at the Little Bighorn Battlefield National Monument. The Indians posed with the tepee were Sioux captives from Slim Buttes, held by the soldiers until reaching the Red Cloud Agency. The photograph was taken by Stanley J. Morrow in late September 1876.

Slim Buttes Battle Monuments. *This obelisk and three soldier burial markers commemorate the Slim Buttes battle in northwestern South Dakota. A roadside marker nearby provides several additional details on the fight.*

GETTING THERE **25**

Slim Buttes Battlefield, South Dakota

When men under Crook's command attacked and systematically burned a Sioux encampment at Slim Buttes on September 9, 1876, they probably did not realize that they were on the Sioux reservation. To get to the battlefield, travel 20.9 miles east on South Dakota 20 from Buffalo. After passing the crest of the Slim Buttes watch for the battle monument and soldier grave markers on the right, near Reva. The battlefield is on private property south and southwest of the markers.

CROOK WITHDREW FROM THE SLIM BUTTES village [25] on the morning of September 10, still under a harassing fire from the Sioux, who were now bolstered by warriors from many nearby Indian camps, including Crazy Horse's. The enfeebled condition of Crook's force prevented him from taking aggressive action, and for the next three days his troops slogged through the cold and rain-soaked prairie toward the Black Hills. The ordeal soon came to be known as the "Starvation March" [26]. In the end the troops had no recourse but to eat their own horses and mules or starve, and the last days on the prairie were cheerless as the exhausted and hungry command toiled southward through thick, clinging mud.

79

Starvation March Country.
*This vast prairie in southwestern North Dakota and
northwestern South Dakota was at its least inviting when
General Crook's Big Horn and Yellowstone Expedition
encountered it in early September 1876. Vegetation is
always sparse, and the chilly fall rains transformed the
landscape into what one campaigner labeled a "ghastly
compound of spongy ashes, yielding sands, and soilless
soulless earth."*

26 GETTING
THERE
Starvation March, South Dakota
From the Slim Buttes Battlefield [25] and Reva, follow South
Dakota 79 south to the Bear Butte State Park [27], approximately
eighty-five miles. The route closely approximates the trail of the Big
Horn and Yellowstone Expedition as it approached the Black Hills.
Having run out of supplies, troops ate their own horses as they marched
toward the mining camps where provisions awaited them. The land-
scape is mixed private and federal property.

RELIEF FROM THE BLACK HILLS MINING COMMUNITIES finally
arrived in Crook's camp on September 13 as the expedition gained the
Belle Fourche River. For several days thereafter the soldiers relished ba-

Haynes Foundation Collection, Montana Historical Society Photograph Archives

Bear Butte.
This ancient volcanic uplift northeast of the Black Hills is a treasured landmark in Indian country. Photograph by F. Jay Haynes.

con, flour, coffee, and an array of other foodstuffs brought forth from Deadwood [5] and Crook City. Ironically, just east of the soldiers' camp loomed the towering Bear Butte [27], one of the most sacred Cheyenne and Lakota landmarks on the northern plains.

GETTING
THERE **27**

Bear Butte, South Dakota

Crook's Starvation March ended just west of what is now Bear Butte State Park, located six miles northeast of Sturgis on South Dakota 79. A park visitor center interprets the sacred butte's continuing role in Cheyenne Indian history. A foot trail to the top of the butte affords a spectacular view of the Starvation March route [26] coming from the north; the Belle Fourche River and Whitewood Creek to the northwest; and the Black Hills to the southwest.

TRAVELER'S TIP: Deadwood [5] and Fort Meade [45] are nearby.

THE BIG HORN AND YELLOWSTONE EXPEDITION recuperated in the Black Hills for a month, proceeding slowly southward until it reached Camp Robinson, Nebraska, [28] on October 22, in time to participate in the disarming and unhorsing of the Red Cloud and Red Leaf Oglala Sioux bands. Disarming all Indians, including those living peaceably at the Sioux agencies, became standard practice in the fall of 1876, as the government asserted heavy-handed control over the Sioux. After witnessing the ordination at Red Cloud Agency [28] of Spotted Tail as head chief of all the Sioux, Crook's Big Horn and Yellowstone Expedition disbanded on October 24. The last of the summer soldiers had retired from the field.

28 GETTING THERE

Camp Robinson and Red Cloud Agency, Nebraska

Crook's Big Horn and Yellowstone Expedition disbanded at what is now Fort Robinson State Park, three miles west of Crawford on U.S. 20. Countless original buildings survive, including many from the 1870s when the post was designated a camp and not a fort. A museum in the 1905 post headquarters features the fort and the Old Army and is the finest of its kind in the American West. The scene of Crazy Horse's death—he was killed in 1877 resisting removal to a Florida prison after the war had ended—is memorialized in several reconstructed buildings and associated monuments. The Red Cloud Agency site is one mile east of the fort on a park road. Established in 1873 for Chief Red Cloud and his Oglala band, as well as for other northern Plains Indians, the agency served as a center for those Indians not at war with the U.S. government in 1876–77. Crazy Horse and his almost nine hundred followers surrendered at Camp Robinson on May 6, 1877. All features are state property.

TRAVELER'S TIP: The 1876 Treaty site [29] is nearby.

AS CAMPAIGNING AGAINST THE SIOUX waged across Wyoming, Montana, and Dakota, the federal government effected a political stratagem that, at least on paper, resolved the so-called Black Hills crisis. In late August a commission chaired by George W. Manypenny commenced levying an ultimatum on the agency Sioux in Nebraska and along the

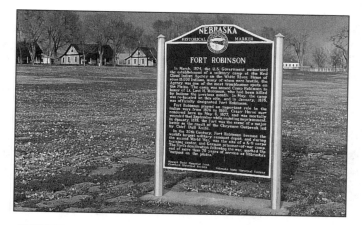

Fort Robinson Marker.

Founded in 1874 and abandoned in 1948, Fort Robinson played a dominant role in the settlement of the American West. Today the fort is a vast historical site featuring dozens of original buildings, many of which have been accurately refurnished; a superlative museum; and numerous monuments and markers commemorating the fort's diverse role in history.

Red Cloud.

The leader of Sioux resistance during the war over the Bozeman Trail in the late 1860s, Red Cloud counseled accommodation to the whites a decade later. A realist, he knew that battlefield gains were temporary and that the old world could not be restored.

U.S. Military Academy

U.S. Military Academy

Camp Robinson in 1877.
*This view, by Fourth Infantry photographer Charles
Howard, shows the sprawling military outpost adjacent to
the Red Cloud Agency. The tent camp in the middle of the
scene was the home of Ranald Mackenzie's Fourth Cavalry
before that regiment departed in the fall for General Crook's
Powder River Expedition.*

Missouri River that forced them to cede the Black Hills and surrounding
hunting lands or lose their rations and even be moved to the Indian
Territory, present-day Oklahoma. With no visible alternative, the agency
people signed. More than a century later, the terms of the so-called Treaty
of 1876 [29] are still argued.

1876 Treaty Monument.
This granite marker in the Crawford city park
commemorates the treaty signing that occurred along the
White River of Nebraska between the Manypenny
Commission and the Oglala Lakotas; the treaty wrested the
Black Hills and hunting lands from the Sioux.

GETTING
THERE **29**

1876 Treaty Site, Nebraska

From U.S. 20 on the immediate west side of Crawford, Nebraska, take First Avenue north to Main Street. Turn left into the Crawford city park. A monument to the 1876 Treaty signing in Nebraska is immediately on the right upon entering the park. Reservation Indians were forced to sign the treaty ceding the Black Hills or face possible removal and the loss of rations. The treaty remains a disputed document.

TRAVELER'S TIP: Camp Robinson and the Red Cloud Agency [28] are nearby.

Chapter IV
The Winter War, 1876–1877

SHERIDAN SAW MILES'S BURGEONING Tongue River Cantonment [24] as the partial fulfillment of his longstanding ambition to establish military posts on the Yellowstone River to protect the coming railroad and cattlemen. He campaigned less stridently for a military presence in the Powder River country, but by mid-October troops were fortifying there as well, establishing Cantonment Reno [30] on the Powder River near old Fort Reno of the Bozeman Trail era [2].

GETTING THERE 30

Cantonment Reno, Wyoming

Cantonment Reno, established in the fall of 1876, served as a forward base for Crook's maneuvering during his winter campaign and as a portentous military presence on the buffalo range. To get to the site, travel east 19.1 miles from Kaycee on Wyoming 192. Turn left onto a county road; signs announce the Bozeman Trail [2] and Fort Reno. Go 5.2 miles. The cantonment site is on the right, nestled in a bend of the Powder River. This is federal property.

TRAVELER'S TIP: The Dull Knife battlefield [34] is nearby.

ON THE YELLOWSTONE, MILES'S NEW POST at the mouth of the Tongue River [24] took shape quickly. The navigation season had ended, and construction materials and winter supplies were stockpiled at Fort Buford [53] at the confluence of the Yellowstone and Missouri rivers, and at the small Glendive Cantonment [31], a remnant of Terry's summer operation. As rapidly as possible, these materials were ushered forward by

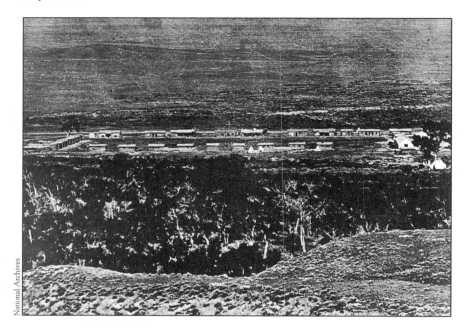

National Archives

Cantonment Reno.
This photograph of Cantonment Reno taken in the fall of 1877 by Charles Howard confirms the camp's plebeian character. The site was abandoned as a military post in mid-1877, but limited use as a way station continued for several more years.

wagon to the Tongue River Cantonment, but in the early going those movements met stern Indian resistance.

On October 10–11 a train of ninety-four wagons escorted by four Twenty-second and Seventeenth infantry companies came under attack at Spring Creek [32], about twenty miles southwest of Glendive [31]. The train returned to Glendive where Otis, in charge, bolstered the escort and resumed the trail to Tongue River [24]. Again, on October 15, in the vicinity of Spring Creek the caravan was attacked by hundreds of warriors. Elwell Otis successfully defended the wagons through the next day in a running fight that covered many miles. When the supply train did not arrive at Tongue River as scheduled, Miles led the entire Fifth Infantry in relief. Otis and Miles united on October 18, and the wagons reached the new cantonment on the twentieth.

Glendive Cantonment Site.
The small army supply camp known as Glendive
Cantonment occupied this Yellowstone River bench opposite
the mouth of Glendive Creek. The shallow undulations of a
redoubt are all that mark the site today.

GETTING
THERE **31**

Glendive Cantonment, Montana

The Glendive Cantonment was used as a way station for supplies bound for the Tongue River Cantonment [24]. A remnant of Terry's summer operation, the small cantonment sat on the west bank of the Yellowstone River, directly opposite the mouth of Glendive Creek. From Interstate 94 at Glendive, take Montana 16 three miles north. Turn right onto a dirt road. In one-half mile the road ends at railroad tracks. The cantonment site, south and southeast of the crossing, was obliterated by railroad construction. Remnants of a redoubt are on the hill, south, above the site. This is private property.

TRAVELER'S TIP: Fort Buford [53] and the Spring Creek skirmish sites [32] are nearby.

32 GETTING THERE — Spring Creek Skirmishes, Montana

The running fights comprising the Spring Creek affair—during which large bands of warriors attacked supplies bound from Glendive [31] to Tongue River [24] in October 1876—occurred on the bench above the Yellowstone between Glendive and Fallon. No actual sites have been identified. Interstate 94 parallels the trail closely and may have obliterated its intermittent traces.

TRAVELER'S TIP: The Glendive Cantonment [31] is nearby.

MILES DID NOT RETURN to his Tongue River post [24], but trailed Otis's attackers into the highlands north of the Yellowstone. On October 20 Miles spotted a large body of Sioux. Two Indians came forward bearing a white flag announcing that Sitting Bull wished to confer with Miles about surrendering his people. The meeting, the first between a government agent and a leader of the non-agency Sioux, was tumultuous

and ultimately fruitless, Sitting Bull declaring his desire to remain in buffalo country and his insistence that the troops must leave. Miles broke off the meeting, and Sitting Bull and his followers returned to their camp five miles away.

Nelson A. Miles.
This portrait of Colonel Nelson Miles of the Fifth Infantry was taken by Stanley J. Morrow at Fort Keogh in 1878. By then, but for Sitting Bull's unsettled residency in Canada, the Great Sioux War was over.

On October 21 Miles advanced against Sitting Bull's village nestled along Cedar Creek [33]. At midmorning the two agreed to talk again, but they could not find mutually satisfying terms. The meeting broke at noon, and Miles deployed for an attack. At first the confrontation resembled a giant chess game, each side seizing minor tactical advantage but neither wishing to fire the first shot. But when the Sioux were seen igniting the grass, Miles's scouts fired and an afternoon-long battle ensued. The Sioux rapidly abandoned their village, fleeing northeast. Casualties in the Cedar Creek engagement included two soldiers wounded and five Indians killed. Like Slim Buttes [25], the village contained Seventh Cavalry relics from the Little Bighorn.

GETTING THERE **33**

Cedar Creek Battlefield, Montana

Five Indians were killed and two U.S. soldiers were wounded at Cedar Creek, when the two sides engaged after stalemated talks between Sitting Bull and Colonel Miles, the first face-to-face meeting to take place between a government agent and a leader of the non-reservation Sioux. To get to the unmarked site, take Prairie County 253 north from Terry. At 16.1 miles turn right onto the Cedar Creek Road, traveling 8.9 miles to a fork. Take the left fork and travel two miles to the site. This is mixed federal and private property.

TRAVELER'S TIP: The Ash Creek Battlefield [35] is nearby.

AS MILES ESTABLISHED HIS RESOLUTE PRESENCE in Montana, General Crook prepared for yet a third assault from the south. Fresh troops again consolidated at Fort Fetterman [7], and the new Powder River Expedition now featured the Fourth Cavalry, commanded by Colonel Ranald S. Mackenzie. Mackenzie, a stern but effective cavalry commander—perhaps Sheridan's best—brought his regiment from Texas and the Indian Territory in August, succeeding Merritt's Fifth Cavalry on Black Hills road patrol. Crook's column marched northward on November 14. While pausing at the new Cantonment Reno [30], scouts reported a large Cheyenne village nestled in the southern Bighorn Mountains. Crook headed there immediately, detaching Mackenzie and the cavalry to close on the camp.

Cedar Creek Battlefield.
The October 1876 clash between Miles's Fifth Infantry and Sitting Bull's Sioux occurred in the ravines and flats in the foreground, near the crest separating the drainages of the Yellowstone and Missouri rivers.

Mackenzie struck the Cheyenne encampment at dawn on November 25, inflicting some of the harshest Indian losses yet in the Great Sioux War [34]. The village, led principally by Morning Star—or Dull Knife, as he was more commonly known—contained 175 lodges and nearly 1,500 Indians, many of whom escaped to the rugged highlands west of the camp. These lodges, too, contained relics from the Little Bighorn battlefield [16], discovered as the camp was being destroyed by the cavalrymen. Soldier casualties in the protracted fight included First Lieutenant John A. McKinney, Fourth Cavalry, and six enlisted men; twenty-six other enlisted men were wounded. Thirty Cheyennes were killed in the battle. Eleven babies froze to death that night, exposed to the frigid weather without shelter. More than any other fight in the Great Sioux War, the ferocity and conclusiveness of the Dull Knife battle demonstrated to the Indians that nothing short of absolute submission would end this war.

Ranald S. Mackenzie.
Colonel of the Fourth Cavalry at the time of the Great Sioux War, Mackenzie was regarded by his mentor, Phil Sheridan, as the finest cavalry commander in the United States Army.

Fort Sill Museum

Nebraska State Historical Society

Little Wolf and Dull Knife.
Patriots of the Northern Cheyennes, Little Wolf (standing) and Dull Knife (also known as Morning Star), had long resisted removal of their bands to the Indian Territory. After surrendering at Camp Robinson in the wake of the Dull Knife battle, however, these tribesmen were transferred south in May 1877.

34 GETTING THERE

Dull Knife Battlefield, Wyoming

The Dull Knife battlefield was the setting for the deadly surprise attack of Mackenzie's cavalry on Morning Star's (or Dull Knife's) village of Cheyennes on November 25. Seven U.S. soldiers and thirty Cheyenne warriors were killed in the fighting, while eleven Cheyenne infants, their shelters destroyed, froze to death the night following the battle.

The Dull Knife battlefield is located west of Kaycee on the Red Fork of the Powder River. West of town, take Wyoming 190 to its end at the hamlet of Barnum. Turn north there traveling a well-established ranch road to its end. The battlefield encompassed the entire bottom land east of the ranch buildings and some of the encircling bluffs. The village was south of the river. An aged monument is just east of the access road near ranch headquarters. This is private property and visitation is not encouraged. Inquire at the Kaycee Museum for seasonal and group visitation opportunities.

TRAVELER'S TIP: The Cantonment Reno site [30] is nearby.

CROOK DISBANDED HIS WINTER CAMPAIGN shortly after the Dull Knife [34] fight. From their Tongue River [24] base, however, Miles's troops continued their harassment of the Sioux. On December 7 during what was known as the Fort Peck Expedition, three Fifth Infantry companies led by First Lieutenant

Dull Knife Battle Monument.
This weathered stone monument on a hillside overlooking the Dull Knife battlefield is the lone on-site marker commemorating the clash between Ranald Mackenzie's Fourth and Fifth Cavalrymen and Dull Knife's Cheyennes.

Dull Knife Battlefield.
Cheyenne leader Dull Knife (Morning Star) was camped at this site along the Red Fork of the Powder River when Colonel Ranald Mackenzie's Fourth Cavalry attacked his village. The Cheyenne camp was nestled amid the trees in the foreground. Many of the Cheyennes escaped to the highlands beyond. Fighting occurred across the landscape.

Frank D. Baldwin attacked Sitting Bull's band as it crossed the Missouri River opposite the mouth of Bark Creek, about eighteen miles below the Fort Peck Indian agency. No casualties were inflicted, and the Indians momentarily eluded their pursuers. But Baldwin again found Sitting Bull's trail midway between the Missouri and Yellowstone rivers and on December 18 attacked his village on Ash Creek [35]. Baldwin captured the camp and destroyed 122 tepees and an abundance of winter provisions. Neither side incurred human casualties, but Sitting Bull's Hunkpapas were again without food and shelter in harsh winter conditions.

Ash Creek Battlefield.
Sitting's Bull's village of Hunkpapa Lakotas was nestled along Ash Creek when a battalion of Fifth Infantrymen led by Frank Baldwin attacked it in early December 1876. The tribesmen escaped but their camp was destroyed.

35 GETTING THERE — Ash Creek Battlefield, Montana

On December 7, three Fifth Infantry companies attacked and destroyed Sitting Bull's camp on Ash Creek, inflicting no human casualties but leaving the Sioux without food or shelter. The Ash Creek site is 7.3 miles beyond the Cedar Creek battlefield [33]. From there continue north. Take the left branch of the wye at 2.8 miles, following the Brockway Road. In another 1.7 miles this road curves westerly. Continue for another 2.1 miles. As the road curves north, with Ash Creek visible to the west, a farm road will be seen trailing west to the creek. The battle monument is visible beyond the ranch buildings above Ash Creek, one mile distant. A road gate may or may not be open or unlocked. This is private property.

TRAVELER'S TIP: The Cedar Creek Battlefield [33] is nearby.

Ash Creek Battle Monument.
This rustic stone pyramid erected in the 1920s overlooks
Ash Creek and the Baldwin–Sitting Bull battle site of
December 1876.

THE DOGGED CAMPAIGNING OF MILES'S "Yellowstone Command"
effectively separated the followers of Sitting Bull from those of Crazy Horse,
preventing any form of coalition that had been the Indians' hallmark the
previous summer. With Sitting Bull contained north of the Yellowstone,
Miles learned at year's end of yet another village, south on the Tongue.
This one, indeed, belonged to Crazy Horse and held refugees from the
Dull Knife battle [34] a month earlier. Miles led seven companies of the
Fifth and Twenty-second infantry into the Wolf Mountains [36] to seek
out the village. As he neared the Indians on January 8, 1877, Crazy Horse
struck and the two forces fought with skill and determination until a blizzard halted the fray at midday. Miles did not pursue the tribesmen, but his
aggressiveness again succeeded in neutralizing a major leader and his followers. Thereafter, diplomatic maneuvering supplanted the battlefield as
the Great Sioux War neared its end.

Courtesy of Jerome A. Greene

Wolf Mountains Battle.
*This woodcut of the January 9, 1877, battle between Miles's
infantry and Crazy Horse's Lakota and Cheyenne warriors
appeared in* Frank Leslie's Illustrated Newspaper *on
May 5, 1877. The field's most prominent landmark, Battle
Butte, is seen at center and is key to locating the site today.*

36 GETTING
THERE
Wolf Mountains Battlefield, Montana
Crazy Horse and Miles clashed in the last large battle of the Sioux
War at the Wolf Mountains battlefield on January 8, 1877. To get to
the site, from Ashland or Lame Deer on U.S. 212 take any of several
roads south to Birney, on the Tongue River. Continue beyond Birney
another 4.8 miles southwest to the battlefield. Cone-shaped Battle
Butte on the right identifies the site, as does a roadside sign. This is
private property.

TRAVELER'S TIP: The Northern Cheyenne Reservation [48]
is nearby.

Chapter V
Sioux War Aftermath, 1877–1881

SITTING BULL TOOK HIS FOLLOWERS TO CANADA in January 1877, where they endured a fitful existence for four and a half years. Many other northern bands simply gave up. Weighing the fruitlessness of continued resistance and the devastating consequences of the Cedar Creek [33], Dull Knife, [34] and Ash Creek [35] battles, the nomadic Sioux began appearing at

Spotted Tail.
Leader of the Brule Lakotas, Spotted Tail was a pragmatist who fully comprehended the fruitlessness of resisting endless white advances into Lakota country. He helped mediate Crazy Horse's surrender in 1877 and for a short while was recognized as chief of all the Sioux. Like several other valiant Lakota leaders, Spotted Tail was murdered, in his case by rival Crow Dog in 1881 on the Rosebud Reservation.

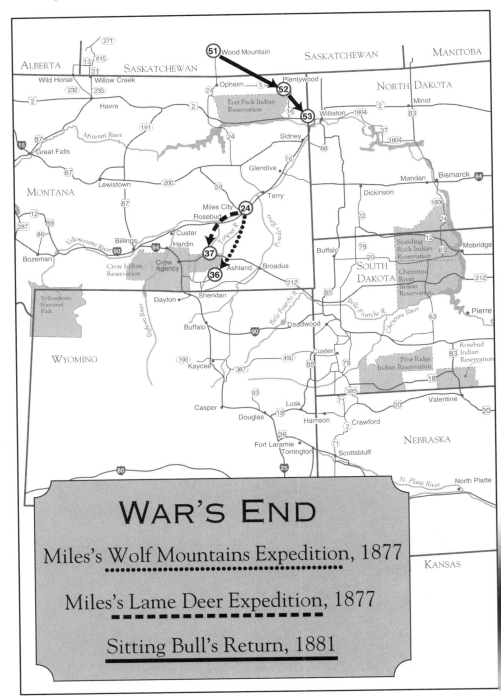

WAR'S END

Miles's Wolf Mountains Expedition, 1877
• •

Miles's Lame Deer Expedition, 1877
▬ ▬ ▬ ▬ ▬ ▬ ▬ ▬ ▬ ▬ ▬ ▬ ▬

Sitting Bull's Return, 1881

Montana Historical Society Photograph Archives

Lame Deer Battlefield.
This photograph taken in 1901 by L. A. Huffman shows the setting of the Lame Deer fight occurring on May 7, 1877. According to Huffman, Lame Deer's village was nestled at the base of the hills seen in the distant center.

their respective agencies in late winter, surrendering their ponies and weaponry as they submitted to government control. The right to hunt in the buffalo country and to possess the Black Hills had been wrested from them by the Manypenny Commission the previous fall. By spring only scattered war-related business remained.

Foremost was the surrender of Crazy Horse and his followers. Chiefs Spotted Tail and Red Cloud both visited Crazy Horse in the spring, speaking frankly but compassionately about the inescapable future. Crazy Horse and his people had suffered terribly that winter and were starving. He finally told Red Cloud that he would come in.

Crazy Horse's surrender was a key closure to the Great Sioux War. With a final impressive display of pageantry, the great leader and his chiefs led a procession of 899 people into the Red Cloud Agency [28] on May 6, 1877. These Oglalas relinquished 117 firearms and 2,200 ponies. More important, Crazy Horse's appearance ended forever an ages-old, nomadic lifestyle. For these Oglalas and all others who had surrendered, the new epoch of acculturation had begun.

A last encounter occurred on May 7 at Muddy Creek, Montana, when Miles's soldiers charged into fifty-one lodges of Minneconjou Lakotas belonging to Lame Deer [37]. Lame Deer had vowed never to surrender, and he and thirteen followers were killed, as were four soldiers. Lame Deer's son, Fast Bull, and 225 others eluded Miles all summer only to surrender at Camp Sheridan, Nebraska, that fall.

37 GETTING THERE

Lame Deer Battlefield, Montana

The final confrontation of the Great Sioux War occurred at the Lame Deer battlefield, when Miles's soldiers attacked Lame Deer's band of Minneconjou Sioux. The modern Lame Deer community has obliterated most traces of the battle site, which was located on the south side of the present town. Remaining undeveloped, however, are the hillsides which served as escape paths for the villagers during the fighting. This is federal property.

TRAVELER'S TIP: Lame Deer is headquarters for the Northern Cheyenne Indian Reservation [48]. As well, Dull Knife is buried in the community cemetery east of the reservation college at the intersection of Montana 39 and U.S. 212. Sitting Bull's sun dance camp [14] is also nearby.

GENERAL SHERIDAN'S NEW MILITARY POSTS on the Yellowstone fully materialized in the summer of 1877, constructed mostly by laborers imported from Minneapolis and St. Paul. Fort Keogh [38] quickly supplanted the crude Tongue River Cantonment [24]. Located on a plain above the Yellowstone about two miles west of Tongue River, Miles's new post insured that Indians would never again control the eastern plains of Montana.

Montana Historical Society Photograph Archives

Spotted Eagle's Sioux Village at Fort Keogh.
This photograph of a bedraggled Sioux village was taken near Fort Keogh by L. A. Huffman in 1880. The occupants had recently surrendered to army agents at the fort after residing in Canada with Sitting Bull since 1877.

GETTING THERE 38

Fort Keogh, Montana

Built in 1877, Fort Keogh replaced the Tongue River Cantonment [24]. It was abandoned in 1908 but reused briefly during World War I. In 1923 the fort was converted into a U.S. Department of Agriculture livestock and range research facility. Though the USDA has consciously obliterated virtually all traces of the historic fort, the flagstaff survives to mark the site. Several officers' quarters have been relocated, including one to the Range Riders Museum at Miles City. The fort site is two miles west of Miles City on Business 94. This is federal property.

Fort Keogh Officers' Quarters.
This 1877 officers' duplex relocated to the grounds of Miles City's Range Riders Museum, is a treasured reminder of the once expansive Fort Keogh. As late as the mid-1980s this and several other identical quarters survived, in original place, on the Fort Keogh grounds, only to be purposefully destroyed by the U.S. Department of Agriculture.

SHERIDAN'S SECOND NEW FORT was located on the bluffs over-looking the confluence of the Little Bighorn and Bighorn rivers, some fourteen miles from the Little Bighorn battlefield **[16]**. Called Bighorn Post and then Fort Custer **[39]**, and for a while renowned as the greatest cavalry station in the nation, the garrison chiefly tended the nearby battle-field and its national cemetery and mediated affairs on the adjacent Crow Indian Reservation.

39 GETTING THERE

Fort Custer, Montana

Built by General Sheridan as a show of force in 1877, Fort Custer was abandoned and fully dismantled in 1898. A commemorative monu-ment marks the site. At the Interstate 90 interchange on the east side of Hardin, follow Montana 313 south across the Bighorn River. Take the first right turn south of the bridge, cross the railroad tracks, and drive to the top of the bluff. The monument is south one-quarter mile. The fort site is in the field on the right. This is private property.

Fort Custer Monument.
*This granite and bronze monument is the lone
commemoration for perhaps the most expansive of the post–
Great Sioux War forts. Today, the fort site is a vast wheat
field, though as recently as the early 1970s the grounds were
not tilled, and the original parade ground and all building
locations were plainly seen.*

SHERIDAN HAD SPENT FOUR YEARS soliciting Congress for
authorization to build forts Keogh [38] and Custer [39]. Other posts came
more easily as the result of the government's desire to contain Sitting
Bull in Canada and the increased seriousness with which Congress took
the Indian threat in the wake of the Great Sioux War. Camp Robinson
[28] became a fort in 1878 and greatly expanded in the 1880s, principally
to oversee the new Pine Ridge Agency [40], just across the border in the
Dakota Territory. Pine Ridge became the postwar home of Red Cloud's
Oglalas, replacing the Red Cloud Agency [28] in Nebraska. Fort Niobrara,
Nebraska [41], was established in 1880, succeeding Camp Sheridan to
provide a watchful presence over the new Rosebud Agency [42], postwar
home of Spotted Tail's Brule Lakotas. Fort Yates, North Dakota [43], was
designated in 1878, a transformation and enlargement of the garrison

guarding the Standing Rock Agency [43], principal home of the Hunkpapa Lakotas. Fort Meade, South Dakota [45], was founded in 1878 northeast of Deadwood [5], serving to buffer the northern Black Hills mining communities from the Sioux. Fort Assinniboine, Montana [46], rose in 1879 in the distant north-central region of that territory, insuring that Sitting Bull's Lakotas would never again reside on American soil as a nomadic people. And Fort McKinney, Wyoming\[49], named for the young army lieutenant killed in the Dull Knife battle [34], was founded in 1877 in the eastern foothills of the Bighorn Mountains, replacing the crude Cantonment Reno [30]. Like Fort Keogh [38] in Montana, McKinney's simple purpose was to insure that the old Powder River buffalo country henceforth belonged to cattlemen, not Indians.

Fort Niobrara.
This stately military post chiefly buffered the settlers and cattlemen of north-central Nebraska from the residents of the Rosebud Sioux Reservation in south-central South Dakota.

Nebraska State Historical Society

THE POSTWAR FORTS AND AGENCIES

Pine Ridge Reservation, South Dakota
GETTING THERE 40

Located on the prairie southeast of the Black Hills, today's Pine Ridge Reservation is a late-nineteenth-century transformation of the Red Cloud Agency [28] after its removal from Nebraska and represents that subdivision of the former Great Sioux Reservation accorded the Oglalas. Reservation headquarters is located at the community of Pine Ridge on U.S. 18.

Fort Niobrara, Nebraska
GETTING THERE 41

Built in 1880 to watch over the Rosebud Agency [42], Fort Niobrara was abandoned in 1906. The site is immediately east of Valentine, on Neb. 12, and is known today as the Fort Niobrara National Wildlife Refuge. The post is commemorated, and a building survives. This is federal property.

Rosebud Reservation, South Dakota
GETTING THERE 42

A transformation of the former Spotted Tail Agency of Nebraska and first called the Rosebud Agency after a small stream by that name, today's Rosebud Indian Reservation in south-central South Dakota is the principal modern-day home of the Brule Lakotas. Reservation headquarters is located in Mission on U.S. 18.

Fort Yates and Standing Rock Reservation, North Dakota
GETTING THERE 43

Designated in 1878 and abandoned in 1903, Fort Yates was on the west bank of the Missouri River, sixty-four miles south of Mandan via North Dakota 1806 and 24. The garrison stationed here supervised the affairs of the Standing Rock Reservation. One army building survives but is unmarked. The surrounding community with the same name is the modern-day headquarters of the Standing Rock Reservation spanning the North Dakota–South Dakota border. Standing Rock is a principal home of the Hunkpapa Lakotas.

TRAVELER'S TIP: Sitting Bull was first buried in the Fort Yates military cemetery, and his initial gravesite is marked on the west side of town. His present gravesite [54] is nearby.

State Historical Society of North Dakota

Fort Yates, North Dakota.
Named for George Yates, an officer killed at the Little Bighorn, this garrison oversaw affairs at the Standing Rock Agency, post-conflict home of many Hunkpapa Lakotas.

Standing Rock Agency.
Almost military in appearance, the Standing Rock Agency buildings seen here in 1880 include an employee residence, left, and the agency school, right. The agency community survives and is known today as Fort Yates, North Dakota, named for the nearby but long defunct military post.

South Dakota State Historical Society

Cheyenne River Reservation, South Dakota

GETTING THERE 44

This subdivision of the former Great Sioux Reservation in the West River Country north of Pierre is the modern-day home of the Minneconjou Lakotas. Eagle Butte is reservation headquarters on U.S. 212.

Fort Meade, South Dakota

GETTING THERE 45

Abandoned as a military post in 1944, Fort Meade is one mile east of Sturgis on South Dakota 34-79, and today has found new life as the Fort Meade Veteran's Hospital. Founded in 1878 to buffer Black Hills mining communities from the Great Sioux Reservation, the post remains nearly intact and features a splendid military museum and cemetery. This is federal property.

TRAVELER'S TIP: The Black Hills mining communities of Custer [4] and Deadwood [5] are nearby, as is Bear Butte [27].

Fort Assinniboine, Montana

GETTING THERE 46

Founded in 1879 to guard against Sioux incursions from Canada, Fort Assinniboine is seven miles southwest of Havre on U.S. 87. Abandoned in 1911, today the fort is a Montana Agricultural Research Center. Many distinctive red-brick buildings survive. This is state property.

TRAVELER'S TIP: The Fort Walsh site [50] is nearby.

Fort Peck Reservation, Montana

GETTING THERE 47

With headquarters at Poplar on U.S. 2, today's Fort Peck Reservation is home to many descendants of Sitting Bull's Hunkpapa Lakotas, along with Assiniboine Indians.

TRAVELER'S TIP: The monument commemorating Sitting Bull's return to Montana [52] is just north of the Fort Peck Reservation at Plentywood, and the site of his formal surrender at Fort Buford [53] is southeast of Bainville.

South Dakota State Historical Society

Fort Meade, South Dakota.
This picture of Fort Meade, with Bear Butte in the background, was taken in the 1880s. Several of these buildings from Fort Meade's early years survive, though most gave way to larger brick structures.

Fort Assinniboine Monument.
This fragile sandstone monument located in front of the original post headquarters commemorates the founding of Fort Assinniboine, Montana, in 1879 by the Eighteenth Infantry. Though this historic marker does not register it, the proper spelling of the post's name is, indeed, Assinniboine.

GETTING
THERE **48**

Northern Cheyenne Reservation, Montana

In the wake of the Great Sioux War, Sitting Bull's and Crazy Horse's Northern Cheyenne allies were summarily removed to the Indian Territory, now Oklahoma. Desiring to live in their traditional homeland, many of the Northern Cheyennes returned heroically to the northern plains in the winter of 1878–79 and were subsequently accorded this reservation in Montana, the headquarters of which is at Lame Deer on U.S. 212.

TRAVELER'S TIP: Reservation headquarters at Lame Deer is central to many sites of the Great Sioux War, including the Rosebud [13], Wolf Mountains [36], and Lame Deer [37] battlefields; Sitting Bull's sun dance camp [14]; and Custer's trail to the Little Bighorn [15].

GETTING
THERE **49**

Fort McKinney, Wyoming

Established in 1877 to replace Cantonment Reno [30], the Fort McKinney site is one mile west of Buffalo on U.S. 16 and currently is occupied by the Wyoming Soldiers and Sailors Home. A highway sign commemorates the fort, abandoned in 1894, and building foundations are visible. This is state property.

TRAVELER'S TIP: The Bozeman Trail [2] is nearby.

AS THE ARMY PROCEEDED TO OCCUPY the former Lakota and Cheyenne Indian country with its new or enlarged military posts, two last episodes, one extraordinarily tragic and the other deeply melancholic, finally concluded the Great Sioux War.

Crazy Horse had not fared well after his surrender in the spring of 1877. Military and civilian authorities at Camp Robinson and Red Cloud Agency [28] feared he would strike for the Powder River country to resume the war or to Sitting Bull's sanctuary in Canada. In midsummer attempts were made to enlist him as a scout against the Nez Perce Indians, who were in the midst of their own flight to Canada, but he would not go.

Courtesy of Tom Buecker

Crazy Horse and Camp Robinson.
This was the setting at Camp Robinson for the tragic death of Crazy Horse on the evening of September 5, 1877. The barrack (left), adjutant's office (center), and guardhouse (right) are reconstructions. The melee occurred at the entrance to the guardhouse.

Crazy Horse Monument.
This large stone pyramid at Fort Robinson commemorates Crazy Horse's legendary life and death. The monument was erected and dedicated in 1934 by the Fort Robinson garrison, in elaborate ceremonies attended by many Indian and white notables.

Fort Walsh.
Founded in 1875 by the North-West Mounted Police, Fort Walsh played a significant role in bringing law to the vast prairie of southern Canada. The fort was reconstructed in the 1940s, and some buildings are refurnished to reflect the era when American Sioux resided in Canada.

Finally, believing that separation was best, General Crook ordered his arrest and removal to a prison in Florida. When beckoned to Camp Robinson on September 5, 1877, Crazy Horse came, but as authorities attempted to incarcerate him he resisted and was mortally bayoneted by Private William Gentles of the Fourteenth Infantry. John G. Bourke, aide to General Crook, offered a simple but poignant eulogy: "As the grave of Custer marked the high-water of Sioux supremacy in the trans-Missouri region, so the grave of Crazy Horse . . . marked the ebb." Directions to Camp Robinson, the site of Crazy Horse's murder, are provided on page 82.

SITTING BULL'S RETURN TO THE UNITED STATES was the war's final, if distant, episode. His years in Canada were fitful. Though his camps once tallied some four thousand Indians scattered from the Cypress Hills in the west to the Wood Mountain [51] in the east, food was scarce and friction common between the American Sioux and the Canadian natives. Prevented from hunting on United States soil by troops from forts Keogh [38] and Assinniboine [46], refugee numbers dwindled until 1881 when on July 19 Sitting Bull and 187 followers surrendered at Fort Buford, Dakota Territory [53]. He had known the Yellowstone-Missouri confluence country well, having traded at nearby Fort Union in his younger years and warred against Fort Buford in the 1860s. But by now the buffalo were nearly gone, and new towns and forts existed. The northern plains no longer belonged to the Sioux.

50 GETTING THERE

Fort Walsh, Saskatchewan

Fort Walsh National Historic Park is one of two sites that bear witness to Sitting Bull's sojourn in Canada. Among many notable events in the fort's history was a meeting held there in October 1877 between Sitting Bull and an American commission led by General Terry. The talks failed, however, as the Sioux brusquely rejected the commission's proposals. Today the park features reconstructed buildings and splendid museum and grounds exhibitry.

Fort Walsh is thirty-two miles (fifty-two kilometers) southwest of Maple Creek on Saskatchewan 271. From Havre, take either Montana 233 or Montana 232 north to the ports of Willow Creek or Wild Horse, respectively. Though longer, the 232 route and its Canadian counterpart is entirely paved and its port of entry open twenty-four hours daily. In Canada, connect with Saskatchewan 13, traveling east to local road 615. Follow 615 north to Saskatchewan 271 and the Fort Walsh National Historic Park. The site is some 120 miles north of Havre. This is federal property.

Wood Mountain Post.
Sitting Bull lived for four years in exile near this 1874
North-West Mounted Police post, which today features
several reconstructed buildings and the timber outlines of
others.

GETTING
THERE 51

Wood Mountain Post, Saskatchewan

In 1874 the North-West Mounted Police acquired buildings and supplies recently surplused by the American–Canadian Boundary Commission. They named their new station Wood Mountain Post after the timbered escarpment nearby. Today the historic site features several reconstructed buildings and the timber outlines of others. Museum exhibitry tells of Sitting Bull's nearby uneasy residency.

The Wood Mountain Post is five miles (eight kilometers) south of Wood Mountain on Saskatchewan 18. To get there from Opheim, Montana, take Montana 24 north to the Port of Opheim, ten miles. Continue north on Saskatchewan 2 to Saskatchewan 18, seven and a half miles, and north again on 18 to the Wood Mountain Post Provincial Historic Park, fifteen miles. This is provincial property.

Sitting Bull Contact Monument. *This scoria and granite monument at the entrance to the Sheridan County Fair Grounds in Plentywood commemorates the return to the United States of Sitting Bull and his followers in July 1881.*

52 GETTING THERE

Sitting Bull Returns to Montana

After four years of struggling in Canada, hunger, conflict with Canadian natives over hunting grounds, and emotional fatigue forced Sitting Bull's surrender to the U.S. Army. Soon after Sitting Bull and his followers crossed the international boundary into Montana in July 1881, they were met by a small delegation of soldiers and outfitters from Fort Buford [53] bearing food and other provisions. This initial contact is commemorated by a small monument along Montana 16 on the east side of Plentywood, Montana.

Fort Buford.

Located at the confluence of the Yellowstone and Missouri rivers, Fort Buford dominated the transportation and settlement activities of the upper Missouri country from 1866 to 1895. Today this original officer quarters, site of Sitting Bull's formal surrender to Major David Brotherton, is carefully refurnished to the era, and other buildings and a museum explore the fort's central role in Dakota and Montana territorial history.

Fort Buford, North Dakota

GETTING THERE **53**

Sitting Bull's formal surrender occurred at Fort Buford's commanding officer's quarters on the west side of the parade ground. To get to the site from Williston, North Dakota, take U.S. 2 seven miles west to North Dakota 1804. Turn south on 1804 and continue sixteen miles to the Fort Buford State Historic Site. Original buildings survive, including the surrender quarters and two containing excellent exhibits. The State Historical Society of North Dakota operates a visitor center nearby and opens the historic buildings seasonally.

From Sidney, Montana, take Montana 200 north through Fairview, twelve miles, to North Dakota 58. Turn north and continue ten miles to North Dakota 1804. Follow local signing to the site. This is state property.

Dull Knife's Grave.
*This is Dull Knife's unpretentious grave in the Lame Deer,
Montana, cemetery. Within the wooden enclosure is also the
grave of Little Wolf, Dull Knife's compatriot in the Northern
Cheyennes' struggle to reserve a Montana homeland.*

IN THE CENTURY SINCE THE CLOSE of the Great Sioux War, the
landscape has healed itself of the blood shed by Lakotas, Cheyennes, and
U.S. soldiers for convictions each believed was right. Today, it is much
easier to appreciate the dramatic beauty of the battlefields than to con-
ceive of their horrors. The same is true for the old forts and towns, whose
remnants speak more easily of triumph than calamity. But this prolonged
saga must always be remembered in human terms. For the most part, for
instance, the soldiers who perished at the Little Bighorn battlefield [16]
are still interred in that hallowed Montana hillside. History reveals less
about the Indian casualties of 1876 and 1877, but it does revere the final
places of the conflict's eminent warriors, both Indian and white. It notes,
for instance, Dull Knife's burial at Lame Deer and Red Cloud's at Pine
Ridge; and Alfred Terry's at Yale University, George Crook's at Arlington
National Cemetery, and George Custer's at the United States Military
Academy.

General Crook's Grave.
This is General George Crook's gravestone in the Arlington National Cemetery, Virginia. A rendition of the well-known photograph by Camillus S. Fly of the general conferring with Geronimo is cast in brass bas-relief on one side.

The record of Crazy Horse's final burial is conflicting. His parents whisked his body from Camp Robinson [28], and some say he was buried along Beaver Creek near Camp Sheridan, Nebraska. Others suggest that it was in the Pine Ridge country of South Dakota. After Sitting Bull's tragic death in 1890 during the ghost dance troubles—he, too, was murdered—his body was buried in the Fort Yates [43] military cemetery, but in 1953 his remains were reinterred in a tranquil setting in north-central South Dakota.

Perhaps of all the places of the Great Sioux War, Sitting Bull's solitary grave [54] atop a bluff overlooking the Missouri River best conveys emotionally the tragedy and triumph of the contest between Indians and whites in the nineteenth century. Death's solitude at Sitting Bull's grave site is powerful, and only the stirring winds break the eerie silence. Sitting Bull's grave has become a place of reflection and an apt epitaph to the Great Sioux War.

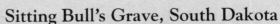

54 GETTING THERE

Sitting Bull's Grave, South Dakota

Reinterred at this solitary site in 1953, Sitting Bull rests in a grave on the west side of Lake Oahe, opposite Mobridge. An obelisk topped by a granite bust carved by Korczak Ziolkowski marks the site. From Mobridge, cross the lake on U.S. 12. In about seven miles turn south, following directional signing to the grave located at pavement's end. This is private property.

Courtesy of Janeen Hedren

Sitting Bull's Grave.
This solitary obelisk along the Missouri River marks Sitting Bull's grave. The remote setting evokes the memory of the Lakotas' struggle to safeguard their homeland in the American West.

Recommended Reading

THE EXTENT OF SCHOLARLY RESEARCH on the Great Sioux War and its chief protagonists is astounding. Among the solid body of modern source material providing both comprehensive analyses of the war's causes and episodes and containing insightful bibliographies for further investigation, these works stand out:

Bray, Kingsley M. *Crazy Horse, A Lakota Life.* Norman: University of Oklahoma Press, 2006.

Greene, Jerome A., ed. *Battles and Skirmishes of the Great Sioux War, 1876–1877: The Military View.* Norman: University of Oklahoma Press, 1993.

————, ed. *Lakota and Cheyenne: Indian Views of the Great Sioux War, 1876–1877.* Norman: University of Oklahoma Press, 1994.

————. *Morning Star Dawn: The Powder River Expedition and the Northern Cheyenne, 1876.* Norman: University of Oklahoma Press, 2003.

————. *Slim Buttes, 1876: An Episode of the Great Sioux War.* Norman: University of Oklahoma Press, 1982.

————. *Stricken Field: The Little Bighorn since 1876.* Norman: University of Oklahoma Press, 2008.

————. *Yellowstone Command: Colonel Nelson A. Miles and the Great Sioux War, 1876–1877.* Lincoln, University of Nebraska Press, 1991.

Hedren, Paul L. *First Scalp for Custer: The Skirmish at Warbonnet Creek, Nebraska, July 17, 1876*. Revised edition. Lincoln: Nebraska State Historical Society, 2005.

—————. *Fort Laramie in 1876: Chronicle of a Frontier Post at War*. Lincoln: University of Nebraska Press, 1988.

—————, ed. *The Great Sioux War 1876–77: The Best from Montana The Magazine of Western History*. Helena: Montana Historical Society Press, 1991.

—————. *We Trailed the Sioux: Enlisted Men Speak on Custer, Crook, and the Great Sioux War*. Mechanicsburg, Penn: Stackpole Books, 2003.

Rankin, Charles E. *Legacy: New Perspectives on the Battle of the Little Bighorn*. Helena: Montana Historical Society Press, 1996.

Robinson III, Charles M. *A Good Year to Die: The Story of the Great Sioux War*. New York: Random House, 1995.

Scott, Douglas D., Richard A. Fox, Jr., Melissa A. Conner, and Dick Harmon. *Archaeological Perspectives on the Battle of the Little Bighorn*. Norman: University of Oklahoma Press, 1989.

Sklenar, Larry. *To Hell with Honor: Custer and the Little Bighorn*. Norman: University of Oklahoma Press, 2000.

Utley, Robert M. *The Lance and the Shield: The Life and Times of Sitting Bull*. New York: Henry Holt and Company, 1993.

Vaughn, J. W. *The Reynolds Campaign on Powder River*. Norman: University of Oklahoma Press, 1961.

—————. *With Crook at the Rosebud*. Harrisburg, Penn.: Stackpole Company, 1956.

INDEX

ABOUT "THE DECISION," BY BILL HOLM

THE DECISION DEPICTS Lieutenant Colonel George Custer the morning of June 25, 1876, as he tried in vain to spot the Sioux and Cheyenne village his scouts had discovered just after dawn. Visibility decreased as the morning grew warmer, and Custer was unable to see signs of the encampment. Nevertheless, he accepted his scouts' insistence that a great Sioux camp lay in the Little Bighorn valley and made a fateful decision to attack at once.

More than a dozen people joined Custer at Crow's Nest, as this location was known, but the artist has shown only Custer, three Crow scouts (White Swan with his telescope, White Man Runs Him, and Goes Ahead), Lieutenant Charles Varnum, chief of Custer's Indian scout detachment, and the civilian scout Charley Reynolds. The painting is based on the actual appearance of the terrain in nearly identical season and atmospheric conditions.

THE AUTHOR

PAUL L. HEDREN retired from the National Park Service in 2007 after a long career spanning assignments in Wyoming, Montana, Utah, North Dakota, and Nebraska. A lifelong student of the Great Sioux War and Black Hills gold rush, Hedren has traveled Sioux Country for more than four decades. He's written or edited seven books, including *With Crook in the Black Hills* (1985), a photo survey of Crook's soldiers passing through the 1876 Dakota gold rush country. Among several current projects, Hedren is completing a book exploring the dramatic changes that enveloped Sioux Country in the late 1870s and 1880s after the warfare ended. He resides in Omaha, Nebraska, where he writes full time.